RETHINKING THE EU BUDGET

RETHINKING THE EU BUDGET

THREE UNAVOIDABLE REFORMS

GABRIELE CIPRIANI

CENTRE FOR EUROPEAN POLICY STUDIES
BRUSSELS

The Centre for European Policy Studies (CEPS) is an independent policy research institute based in Brussels. Its mission is to produce sound analytical research leading to constructive solutions to the challenges facing Europe today. CEPS Paperbacks present analysis and views by leading experts on important questions in the arena of European public policy. They are written in a style geared to an informed but generalist readership of policy-makers, government officials and corporate executives.

The author of this book, Gabriele Cipriani, is an official of the European Court of Auditors. The views expressed here represent exclusively the position of the author and do not necessarily correspond to those of any institution with which he is associated. He gratefully acknowledges insightful comments as well as helpful research and editorial assistance received, which have greatly contributed to this book.

ISBN 978-92-9079-735-7

Centre for European Policy Studies
Place du Congrès 1, B-1000 Brussels
Tel: 32 (0) 2 229.39.11 Fax: 32 (0) 2 219.41.51
e-mail: info@ceps.be
internet: http://www.ceps.eu

CONTENTS

List of Figures

List of Tables

List of Boxes

PREFACE

Several institutional actors and academic experts have highlighted the inadequacy of the present EU budget to fulfil the objectives set and to deliver the outcomes it is expected to produce. The full, wide-ranging review of the EU budget requested by the European Council in December 2005, due to be finalised in 2008–09, is at once an opportunity and a difficult challenge, unpredictable in its result.

Many are the issues that are deemed to undergo scrutiny. The present EU budget concentrates its resources on two main policies whilst funding simultaneously, in a variety of sectors, dozens of programmes with reduced appropriations. It has a revenue system characterised by numerous specific arrangements accumulated over the years, which nevertheless provides the financial resources required but has no link with the taxpayer. The EU budget is framed in a seven-year financial perspective that allows little flexibility and limited opportunity for ongoing corrective action. It finances policies that are not really designed to achieve specific and identifiable results, while spending is an implicit objective. Finally, the EU budget is implemented for the most part in shared management with the member states, with a consequent weak accountability given the numerous actors involved, each of them with different responsibilities.

These weaknesses are not attributable to a supposedly wrong conceptual design, but rather derive from the EU integration process. Behind the scenes, sensitive matters such as the unanimity rule, the institutional balance of powers between the European institutions and the role of national parliaments are at stake. As such, the EU budget is a key condition for the evolution of European integration and part of the debate about the legitimacy of the Union's actions. Yet it cannot remain an issue among governments alone. In this respect, it is to be welcomed that the Commission has just launched a broad consultation to stimulate an open debate on the EU's finances. Indeed, to debate the EU budget is actually to discuss visions of Europe's future.

Against this background, this study identifies three reforms that seem a precondition for progress. These are the setting-up of a single revenue system for all member states, the clear identification of specific and verifiable objectives for the programmes financed and, finally, the achievement of full accountability for the implementation of the budget.

Gabriele Cipriani
November 2007

Not everything that counts can be counted,
and not everything that can be counted counts.

Albert Einstein

1. THE EU BUDGET – AN HISTORICAL RELIC?

In 1978, the European Commission acknowledged that the Community budget "reflects the reality of a very partial and extremely localised financial integration", being "neither a true instrument for financing a wide range of policies nor a means of redistribution worthy of the name, nor an instrument of economic stabilisation".[1] This statement must still be valid in its essence if, more than 25 years later, the Commission could conclude that the European Union "should commit itself to carrying out a comprehensive review of all aspects of the organisation of the EU budget – expenditure, revenue and structure – with a view to ensuring that the budget is equipped to respond to the challenges of the future".[2] The European Council also seems to have been convinced of the need to carry out a comprehensive reassessment of the financial framework, when it called on the Commission "to undertake a full, wide ranging review covering all aspects of European Union spending, including the CAP [Common Agricultural Policy], and of resources, including the UK's rebate, to report in 2008/9".[3]

---

[1] See European Commission, *Global appraisal of the budgetary problems of the Community*, COM(78) 64, Brussels, 27 February 1978, p. 2.

[2] See European Commission, "Five proposals to relaunch negotiations", Memo/05/386, Brussels, 20 October 2005(a).

[3] See European Council, *Financial Perspective 2007-2013*, 15915/05, Brussels, 19 December 2005(a), paras 79–80. The Interinstitutional Agreement on budgetary discipline and sound financial management of 17 May 2006 between the European Parliament, the Council and the Commission provides (Declaration No. 3) that the

Such statements do not come as a surprise to the academic world. For years, there has been a large identity of views among academic experts about the inadequacy of the present EU budget to fulfil the objectives set and to deliver the outcomes it is expected to produce.[4] The conclusions of the Sapir et al. report (2003) are unambiguous in this respect:

> As it stands today, the EU budget is a historical relic. Expenditures, revenues and procedures are all inconsistent with the present and future state of EU integration. Half its spending goes on supporting a sector whose economic significance is declining, little is used to provide economic or non-economic public goods typically featuring large economies of scale, while convergence policy is very dispersed across EU countries and is not focused regarding the activities it should support.[5]

Indeed, academia is at one in stating:

- The financing of the CAP by the EU budget no longer seems justified (and much less when it takes up around one-third of the budget), because the CAP has "moved away from being an allocative policy, promoting efficiency and production, towards being a distributive

---

European Parliament will be associated with the review at all stages of the procedure and will be part of any formal follow-up steps (see European Parliament, Council and Commission, Interinstitutional Agreement between the European Parliament, the Council and the Commission of 17 May 2006 on budgetary discipline and sound financial management, OJ C 139/1, 14.6.2006).

[4] See for example, Tabellini (2002), Sapir et al. (2003), Buti & Nava (2003), Begg (2004 and 2005), Baldwin (2005) and Gros & Micossi (2005).

[5] The report went on to say,

> More than 90% of the EU budget is financed through national contributions linked to national treasuries, rather than from taxes levied on EU-wide fiscal bases.

> Finally, the procedure for adopting the EU Financial Perspectives (the multi-annual frameworks, which determine the maximum amount for every item of expenditure in the EU annual budget) is driven by narrow national calculations of self-interest, bolstered by unanimity voting. (Sapir et al., 2003, p. 172)

Prof. André Sapir chaired a High-Level Group invited by the then President of the European Commission, Romano Prodi, to review the entire system of EU economic policies and to propose a strategy for delivering faster growth together with stability and cohesion in the enlarged Union.

policy for a particular group of citizens".[6] Instead, policies promoting economic growth within the EU area – research & development (R&D), innovation, education and training, and infrastructure – should be given priority, especially now that this need is recognised by the Lisbon strategy.[7]

- Cohesion policy should be refocused. To reduce the range of income disparities across EU countries brought about by enlargement, regional convergence funds should be allocated to low-income countries in need of above-average growth in order to converge towards the rest of the EU. Therefore, structural policies should be concentrated on genuinely poor countries (in other words, the new member states from Eastern Europe), rather than on poor regions of relatively rich countries (the old 15 member states or EU-15).

- The financing of the EU budget should be rationalised and exceptions should be avoided, above all the UK rebate.[8] A choice should be made between a system of national contributions and an EU-based tax, thus

---

[6] Ibid., p. 164. For a description of the CAP reform see European Commission, "EU fundamentally reforms its farm policy to accomplish sustainable farming in Europe", Press release, IP/03/898, Brussels, 26 June 2003(a).

[7] At the Lisbon summit in March 2000, the European Council set out a strategy to make Europe the most competitive economy in the world. The Lisbon strategy consists of three pillars (economic, social and environmental) and covers a very wide range of policies. The Lisbon summit set the target of achieving far-reaching reforms at the European and national levels in areas such as macroeconomic policy, enterprise, R&D, opening markets and the environment. After initially modest results, the strategy was relaunched in spring 2005. The European Council agreed to refocus priorities on jobs and growth consistent with the sustainable development strategy, by mobilising to a greater degree all appropriate national and Community resources. Two headline targets have been set: investment of 3% of Europe's GDP in R&D by 2010 and an employment rate (the proportion of Europe's working age population in employment) of 70% by the same date, which is equivalent to the creation of 20 million jobs. For the implementation of the Community Lisbon programme, see the European Commission's report, Communication on Implementing the Renewed Lisbon Strategy for Growth and Jobs: "A year of delivery", COM(2006) 816, Brussels, 12 December 2006(a).

[8] The UK has benefited, since 1980, from a reduction in its budgetary burden under various forms. See the section "The UK rebate, at the crossroads of any reform".

at least weakening the endless debate about net-payer and net-recipient member states.

'Financial perspective': Whose perspective?

When considering the revenue side, the EU budget is objectively in an unenviable situation, unknown elsewhere in any member state. The financial resources are guaranteed whatever happens, and any form of 'tax avoidance' is unimaginable. This is because the EU budget is financed by the member states, which have an obligation to make the corresponding funding available.[9] That is not to say, however, that the resources made available to the EU budget are unlimited. Member states have decided that a ceiling equal to 1.24% of the sum of member states' gross national income (GNI)[10] should apply. That means an amount of around €120 billion a year.

---

[9] Art. 269 of the Treaty establishing the European Community (EC Treaty or TEC) (2006 consolidated version as amended by the Treaty of Nice) establishes an absolute obligation in this respect. For example, when owing to exhaustion of the own resources a shortfall in revenue appeared in 1984 and 1985, transitional financing solutions were applied and member states contributed supplementary amounts to cover the deficit. The Own Resources Decision implements Art. 269 TEC. The Decision establishes in particular the global ceiling on the own resources, the typology of the resources financing the budget and the burden-sharing arrangements among member states. The Decision has first to be unanimously adopted by the EU Council of Ministers and, to come into force, requires ratification by the member states according to their own constitutional rules (for the period 2007–13, the Council's Decision 2007/436/EC, Euratom of 7 June 2007 on the system of the European Communities' own resources, OJ L 163, 23.6.2007, is not yet in force, pending ratification). Hence, the Own Resources Decision constitutes in practice a treaty within the EC Treaty. It should be noted that the European Parliament can only give an opinion on this Decision. This is the consequence of the respective powers of the two arms of the EU budgetary authority (the European Parliament and the Council) outlined by Art. 272 TEC. Para. 10 of Art. 272 recalls that each institution shall exercise the powers conferred upon it by the Treaty, especially those relating to the Communities' own resources and to the balance between revenue and expenditure.

[10] GNI is equal to gross domestic product (GDP) minus primary income payable by resident units to non-resident units, plus primary income receivable by resident units from the rest of the world. The GNI and GDP aggregates form part of the definitions laid down in the European System of Integrated Economic Accounts (ESA 95) adopted by Council Regulation (EC) No. 2223/96 of 25 June 1996 on the

Other limitations are applicable to the EU budget. Revenue and payment appropriations must be in balance (the principle of equilibrium)[11] and the EU may not raise loans.[12]

Yet the main constraint is the so-called 'financial perspective', which was first introduced in 1988 to prevent previously recurring budgetary crises.[13] This multi-annual framework, which is actually not foreseen in either the Treaty or Community legislation,[14] arises from an Interinstitutional Agreement between the institutions involved in the budgetary cycle (the European Parliament, Council and Commission), which gives credibility to the mechanism.

European system of national and regional accounts in the Community (OJ L 310, 30.11.1996). In the framework of the EU budget, the concept of GNI replaced the concept of gross national product (GNP) as of 2002. The concept of GNP applied under the ESA second edition statistical system is conceptually identical to the definition of GNI under the ESA 95. The problems with using GNI in the EU context are examined in the section "In need of more than one GNI?".

[11] See Art. 268 TEC. The situation was different under the Treaty establishing the European Coal and Steel Community (ECSC Treaty) (1951), where the principle of equilibrium was applied over a number of years, with the result that annual imbalances were allowed.

[12] The Financial Regulation (Council Regulation (EC, Euratom) No. 1605/2002 of 25 June 2002 on the Financial Regulation applicable to the general budget of the European Communities, OJ L 248, 16.9.2002) as amended by Regulation No. 1995/2006 of 13 December 2006 (OJ L 390, 30.12.2006) emphasises "that recourse to loans is not compatible with the system of Community own resources" (see the ninth successive para. introduced by "Whereas" and Art. 14(2)).

[13] The other bulwark in this context is Art. 270 TEC, introduced in 1992 by the Treaty on European Union (Maastricht Treaty). According to this provision, the Commission shall not make any proposal for a Community act, alter its proposals or adopt any implementing measure that is likely to have appreciable implications for the budget without providing the assurance that that proposal or that measure is capable of being financed within the limit of the Community's own resources.

[14] Once ratified, the new reform Treaty for Europe, agreed by EU heads of state and government in Lisbon (18-19 October 2007), will modify the EC treaty by introducing the principle of establishing a multi-annual financial framework (for at least five years), to be decided by the Council after obtaining the agreement of the European Parliament (see article 270a of the draft treaty, http://www.consilium.europa.eu/uedocs/cmsUpload/cg00001re01en.pdf).

Financial perspectives aim at guaranteeing financial discipline and an orderly development of expenditure.[15] This framework sets the spheres of activity of the EU budget and the amounts devoted to each big spending area (agriculture, structural policies, internal policies,[16] external actions,[17] administrative expenditure and reserves) and it fixes the limits of EU expenditure for seven years.[18] Little flexibility is allowed (see Box 1.1).

---

[15] Limitations on the growth of expenditure are set by category for commitment appropriations and on total expenditure for payment appropriations. The distinction between commitment and payment appropriations ('differentiated appropriations') is a peculiarity of the EU budget that has to reconcile the principle of annuality with the need to engage in multi-annual operations (notably for structural policies). This distinction goes back to Art. 176(1) of the Treaty establishing the European Atomic Energy Community (Euratom Treaty) (1957) and was given widespread application by Art. 7 of the Financial Regulation.

- Commitment appropriations make it possible to enter into legal obligations during the financial year in respect of operations to be carried out over a period of more than one financial year.

- Payment appropriations make it possible to cover expenditure, up to the amount entered in the budget, arising from commitments entered into during the financial year or in previous financial years (or both).

[16] Internal policies cover a wide range of activities contributing to the development of the single market. More than half relates to research and technological development. Other areas of intervention are consumers, the internal market, industry and networks, training, youth and social operations, energy, Euratom and the environment.

[17] External policies deal with external aid (mainly food aid, food security, humanitarian aid, the co-financing of non-governmental organisations and relations with third countries) as well as the pre-accession strategy covering expenditure for Central and Eastern European countries and Turkey.

[18] For reasons of democratic responsibility and accountability, the European Parliament has pleaded in favour of a parallelism between the duration of the financial perspective and the five-year mandates of the European Parliament and of the Commission (see European Parliament, Resolution of 8 June 2005 on Policy Challenges and Budgetary Means of the Enlarged Union 2007–13, para. 33).

Box 1.1   Financial perspective

In the event of unforeseen circumstances, the Commission may propose a revision of the financial perspective. Yet the maximum level of financing of the EU budget must still respect the ceilings defined in the Own Resources Decision (1.24% of GNI for payments and 1.31% in commitments). A decision to revise the financial framework is taken jointly by the Council and the European Parliament. When this revision does not exceed 0.03% of the EU GNI, agreement requires a qualified majority in the Council and a vote of the European Parliament by a majority of its members and three-fifths of the votes cast. If the revision is above 0.03% of the EU GNI, the Council needs to act unanimously (see European Parliament, Council and Commission, 2006, Art. 22). A number of instruments are already available outside expenditure ceilings agreed in the financial framework to face unforeseen events. They include:

- the EU solidarity fund (maximum €1 billion per year in current prices), created in 2002 to provide rapid financial support in the event of major disasters;

- the Instrument of Flexibility (maximum €200 million per year in current prices), intended to allow the financing of clearly identified expenditure that could not be financed within the limits of the ceilings available for one or more other headings. This instrument has been used intensively in the past, notably as an indirect means to raise the ceiling for external actions;

- the emergency aid reserve (maximum €1,744 million for the whole period, at current prices), to provide a rapid response to the specific aid requirements of non-member countries following events that could not be foreseen when the budget was established, chiefly for humanitarian operations;

- in addition, it is possible to mobilise the European globalisation adjustment fund (maximum €500 million per year in current prices) by using unused appropriations from the previous year. The fund is intended to enable the Community to provide support for workers made redundant as a result of major structural changes in world trade patterns where these redundancies have a significant adverse impact on the regional or local economy; and

- finally, an amount of €564 million for the whole period (at current prices) is foreseen for administrative expenditure.

By setting binding, long-term spending ceilings for the main categories of EU expenditure, the financial perspective establishes the expenditure for each of the years and for each heading or subheading. The annual ceilings apply to each financial year and they may in no way be aggregated over the period. Indeed, the institutions acknowledge that each of the absolute amounts shown in the financial framework represents an annual ceiling on expenditure under the EU budget. The consequence is that the annual EU budget becomes a subsidiary instrument of the multi-annual framework. It remains instrumental in its implementation and is indeed largely predictable.

As shown by Figure 1.1, the Council (and thus the member states) largely dominates the financial framework, as a consequence of its absolute power over the resources to be allocated to the EU budget.[19]

Figure 1.1 Adoption of the 2006 EU budget (payment appropriations) (€ billion)

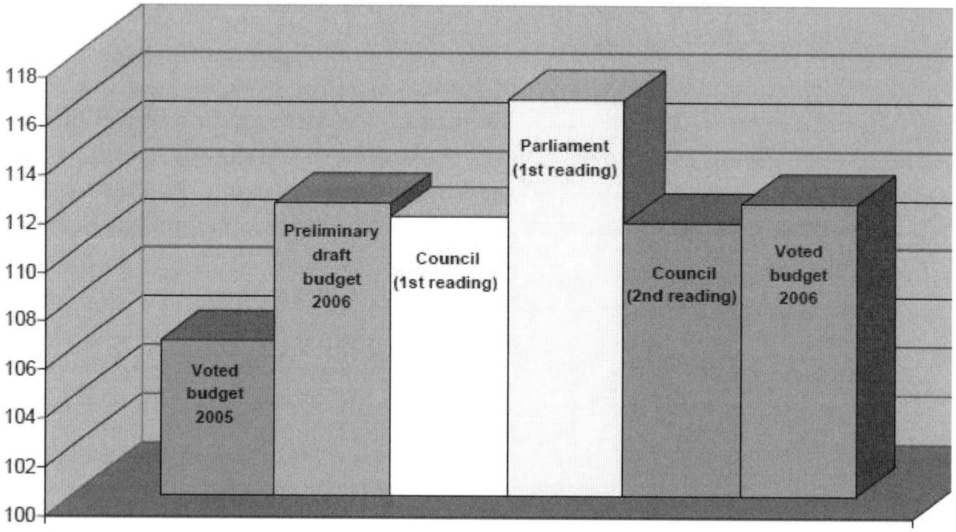

Source: European Commission (2006i).

The first two financial perspectives were characterised by significant increases in appropriations, especially owing to the development of the

---

[19] Indeed, the Council's website reminds visitors that "[t]he Council is the main decision-making body of the European Union". See also footnote 9.

structural policies and the accession of Spain and Portugal to the EU. For the period 1988–92, the overall ceiling was gradually increased from 1.15% of GNP for 1988 to 1.20% for 1992.

A further increase (from 1.24% to 1.27% of GNP) was agreed for the period 1993–99. During this period, there was an especially significant development of the structural policies, as economic and social cohesion became a pre-condition for creating the single European currency.

Since 2000, the tendency has been rather in the direction of the stabilisation of expenditure. For both financial perspectives, 2000–06 and 2007–13, the same overall own resources ceiling has applied (1.24% of GNI).[20] This ceiling has been maintained despite the unprecedented challenge to the competitiveness and internal cohesion of the Union represented by the accession to the EU of ten new member states in 2004 and two more as of 1 January 2007. It is also notwithstanding the fact that in the enlarged Union, average GDP per capita is now more than 12% lower than in the EU-15, and income disparities have doubled overall.[21]

The financial perspective for 2007–13 sets the global level of commitment appropriations at €864.3 billion (2004 prices),[22] equal to 1.05%

---

[20] Although conceptually identical, total GNI is higher in volume than total GNP (1.24% of GNI is equal to 1.27% of GNP). For the details of this equivalence see European Commission, Communication on adaptation of the ceiling of own resources and of the ceiling for appropriations for commitments following the entry into force of Council Decision 2000/597/EC, Euratom, COM(2001) 801, Brussels, 28 December 2001. It should be noted that the Own Resources Decision (Council Decision 2000/597/EC, Euratom of 29 September 2000 on the system of the European Communities' own resources, OJ L 253, 7.10.2000) established the principle (in the seventh successive para. introduced by "Whereas") that the change in the reference aggregate from GNP to GNI should not increase the amount of financial resources put at the disposal of the Communities. The ceiling of own resources had therefore to be adjusted downwards. See also footnote 176.

[21] See European Commission, *Building our common future: Policy challenges and budgetary means of the enlarged Union 2007–13*, COM(2004) 101, Brussels, 26 February 2004(a), p. 15.

[22] As far as the global level of commitment appropriations for the period is concerned, it should be recalled that the Commission's proposal was for €1,022.4 billion (1.24% of EU GNI – 2004 prices). The European Parliament asked in June 2005 for a lower amount (€974.8 billion, or 1.18% of EU GNI – 2004 prices). The Council reached agreement in December 2005 at €862.4 billion (1.045% of EU GNI –

of EU GNI. Total payment appropriations have been fixed at a lower level, €820.8 billion (2004 prices), and equal to 1.00% of EU GNI. This means that, by reference to the 1.24% of the EU GNI ceiling, €197 billion of further expenditure remains theoretically possible. A revision of the financial perspective would be required, however.[23]

As shown in Table 1.1, agricultural (heading 2) and structural policies (heading 1b)) continue to take up the lion's share of expenditure (nearly 80%).

2004 prices). Compared with this last figure, the final compromise set in the Interinstitutional Agreement entails a supplementary €2 billion (essentially for competitiveness for growth and employment), plus a further €2 billion outside the expenditure ceilings.

[23] The 2007–13 financial perspective does not include EU expenditure on financial and technical cooperation with developing countries under the European development fund (EDF), which, as in the past, will continue to fall outside the EU budget. The EDF represents appropriations equal to around 0.03% of GNI. The financial provisions of the current EDF (9th EDF) expire at the end of 2007. For the period 2008–13 member states have agreed global expenditure of €22.7 billion (current prices). The proposal to integrate the EDF into the EU budget dates back to 1973 and it was reiterated by the Commission in February 2004. This expenditure will continue to be funded through separate contributions by the member states. This is because the cost-sharing formula, reflecting the special relations between certain member states and the beneficiary countries, is different from that used to determine the expenditure of the general budget. For example, the UK, Spain and Ireland opposed the integration of the EDF in the EU budget as of 2007 because this would have increased their financial contribution (on the EDF financial and management peculiarities, see European Commission, 2002a, chapter 17). Further evidence of member states' different interests is provided by the setting-up, in April 2007, of a trust fund for the development of major infrastructure networks in Africa, with an initial allocation (2006–07) of €87 million, of which €27 million is provided by nine member states (Germany, Austria, Belgium, Spain, France, Greece, Italy, Luxembourg and the Netherlands) and the balance by the EDF.

Table 1.1 Financial perspective 2007–13 (€ billion)

Heading	€ Billion (2004 prices)	% of Total
1. Sustainable growth	382.1	44.2
a) Competitiveness for growth and employment	74.1	8.6
b) Cohesion for growth and employment	308.0	35.6
2. Preservation & management of natural resources	371.3	43.0
3. Citizenship, freedom, security and justice	10.8	1.2
a) Freedom, security and justice	6.6	0.8
b) Citizenship	4.1	0.5
4. The EU as a global player	49.5	5.7
5. Administration and other	49.8	5.8
6. Compensations	0.8	0.1
Total for 2007–13	864.3	100.0

Source: European Commission (2006j).

Concluding remarks

The financial perspective has fully played its role of straitjacket and expenditure stabiliser, in both absolute volume and for each of the different spending headings. Yet these two objectives are not interdependent, as the limitation on the volume of resources for the EU budget could be ensured by the own resources ceiling alone. Instead, ways of ensuring greater freedom concerning the expenditure headings of the financial perspective could be explored, for example by relaxing the current practice of committing the whole appropriations at the beginning of the financial perspective (in particular for structural policies). This step would facilitate taking account of new emerging priorities and permit the necessary corrective action in the programmes decided. Not least, it would enhance the meaningfulness of the annual budgetary procedure.

Is the size of the budget a major issue?

The EU Treaty establishes that "[t]he Union shall provide itself with the means necessary to attain its objectives and carry through its policies".[24] Concerning the EU budget, it is often observed that it is too small as it corresponds to 'only' slightly more than 1% of member states' joint GDP, while for example the federal budget of the United States represents the equivalent of some 20% of US GDP and that of Canada some 18%. Comparisons are also made with the member states' budgets, which take up an average of around 48% of national income. The MacDougal report had already suggested in 1997 that in order to have a perceptible macroeconomic effect on the Community economy as a whole, the minimum volume of the EU budget should be 2 to 2.5% of member states' joint GDP.[25]

The evolution of the EU budget has been completely different, as shown by Figure 1.2. Three elements may be highlighted:

- EU expenditure was relatively stable in the period considered. It represented around 1% of EU GDP. Both the stability and volume of funds are attributable to the straitjacket of the financial perspective that governs EU expenditure. For the same reason, no significant change should be expected at least until 2013.

- The trends of EU and national expenditure were different and clearly asymmetric for some years. Still, this seems of little relevance, given the huge differences in the order of magnitude of the appropriations (and of the policies covered). In addition, unlike the EU budget, national budgets are not bound by a 'financial perspective' or by the principle of equilibrium between revenue and expenditure.

- The annual increase of EU expenditure also participated in the trend towards a general rise in public expenditure greater than that of real GDP growth, although again without a causality link over time.

---

[24] See Art. 6(4) of the Treaty on European Union (signed in Maastricht, 1992).
[25] See European Commission (1977), p. 17.

Figure 1.2 EU expenditure and EU national expenditure 1996–2006

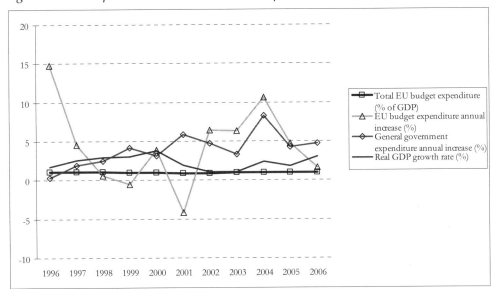

Note: Data is for the EU-15 for 1996–2003 and for the EU-25 for 2004–06.

Source: Own calculations based on European Commission (2007l) and Eurostat data.

When examining whether the present size of the EU budget is or is not sufficient, one should be aware that the appropriations already available by applying the own resources ceiling of 1.24% of GNI are usually not fully used. As has been stressed by the European Parliament, "no budget has ever come close to this ceiling…with payment appropriations reaching their maximum level in 1993 at 1.18% of GNP". Had this ceiling been fully used, the EU "budget would have gained an annual 0.2% of GNI over the last 13 years, equivalent to an increase of approximately EUR 240 billion".[26] As confirmation of the above, the 2007 budget foresees expenditure equal to 0.99% of the GNI, while the financial perspective for 2007–13 would authorise a rate of 1.06% of GNI.

Moreover, the slow process of actually disbursing the funds for operations managed over a number of years, i.e. structural policies and internal policies as well as external policies, makes a surplus of the EU

---

[26] See European Parliament, Resolution of 29 March 2007 on the future of the European Union's own resources, paras 8 and 32.

budget at year-end a normal occurrence.[27] Between 1999 and 2003, under-spending caused cancellations of almost €40 billion of payment appropriations.

The evolution of EU expenditure is essentially determined by how fast the programmes are carried out (by the member states, in the case of structural policies), a factor over which the Commission has de facto little influence, except by purely cancelling the funds allocated.[28] If a certain amount of outstanding payments is normal owing to the multi-annual nature of several programmes, one should note that at the end of 2006 outstanding payments reached €132 billion (some 11% more as compared with 2005).[29] Structural policies accounted for about 70% of this amount, which represented as a whole 2.6 years of payments (at the 2006 spending rate). One could also notice that at the end of the 2000–06 programming

---

[27] Art. 268 TEC requires the budget to be balanced each year. An annual surplus is entered into the budget for the following year, reducing the revenue required from member states (see also footnote 11). In recent years, the surplus went from €11.6 billion in 2000 to €2.4 billion in 2005 and €1.9 billion in 2006. Yet, this was because of a significant reduction of payment appropriations during the year (€4.6 billion in 2006), anticipating lower than expected spending in agricultural and structural policies. For the period 2007–13, there is a risk that the surplus will increase again until new programmes have reached their cruising speed.

[28] For example, according to the rules applicable to structural policies, the Commission can decommit the amounts committed in year n for programmes for which no justified payment claim is presented by the end of year $n+2$ ($n+3$ for those member states – the new member states, Greece and Portugal – whose GDP from 2001 to 2003 was below 85% of the EU-25 average in the same period). Such decommitments remain limited (less than 1%) in comparison with average annual commitments. In 2005, €286 million was decommitted (slightly over the €254 million of 2004). A significant share (44%) was related to the European social fund operations. A lower amount was decommitted in 2006 (€217 million).

[29] In this respect, one should note an increasing trend of outstanding payments, mostly owing to structural policies (and the cohesion fund in particular). As a matter of comparison, the increase between year-end 2005 and year-end 2006 was + 14% (+ 23% for the cohesion fund). In particular, the enlargement countries record a low absorbing rate for structural funds. Yet, approximately half of the €347 billion worth of 2007–13 cohesion spending is intended for the new member states.

period, an amount of 28% remained to be paid.[30] This will be in addition to the payments for the new programming period.

As has been observed by the European Court of Auditors, "it is contradictory to increase the budget each year when there is not the ability to absorb the resources on multi-annual programmes within the timescale foreseen",[31] not to mention that an accumulation of unspent commitments inevitably increases the risk in terms of the quality of spending. One can indeed imagine the pressure that would be brought to bear on member states (by their own citizens) and on the Commission (through criticism from the European Parliament) if Community funds were to remain unused.[32]

Figure 1.3 shows that outstanding commitments[33] have risen faster than the budget.

Figure 1.3 Outstanding budgetary commitments 1994–2006 (€ billion)

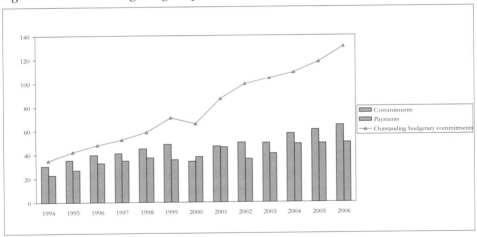

Source: European Court of Auditors (2007c), Graph 3.1.

---

[30] This level of outstanding payments is significantly higher (+30%) compared with the situation in 1999, at the end of the previous programming period.

[31] See European Court of Auditors, *Annual Report concerning the financial year 2003*, OJ C 293, 30.11.2004, para. 2.49. A similar observation has been made by the Court in its 2006 Annual Report (2007c), para. 3.20.

[32] Concerning specifically the European Parliament, see footnote 98.

[33] The reference here is to differentiated appropriations (for a definition see footnote 15), which comprise expenditure on structural policies, internal policies, external actions and pre-accession aid.

Concluding remarks

There are grounds for wondering whether the present EU financial and management framework, which is to a large extent dependent upon the administrative capacity of the member states to implement EU agricultural and structural policies, could actually cope with a substantial increase of appropriations. This consideration also shows that, given the different functions assigned to these budgets and the different share of responsibilities between central and local levels, comparisons with the size of federal states' budgets or those of the EU member states in general are not in themselves an appropriate scale of reference. There is actually no 'ideal' or 'normal' size for the EU budget as such. Whether the EU budget is too small or not is basically a question that is only relevant once the objectives to meet have been set. As the Commission has said in the context of future enlargements, "[T]he Union needs to ensure…that its budget is commensurate with its objectives and with its financial resources."[34] What matters is what it is intended to achieve. The size of the EU budget ought naturally to be determined by the sum of the costs of the various policies assigned to the EU. If the 'volume' of funds is an issue, this is much more at the programme level than for the EU budget as a whole.

A panoply of programmes

The Commission's proposal concerning the 2007–13 financial framework aimed at a reorientation of expenditure in favour of policies fostering growth and employment. It was made clear, however, that the evolution of expenditure for the period 2007–13 had already been largely determined.[35] On one hand, market-related and direct payments on agriculture had been previously agreed until 2013[36] and, on the other hand, the significantly lower level of prosperity in the new member states required increased expenditure on cohesion. Taking account also of the requirements of the other policies, the Commission therefore concluded that "a ceiling around 1% of GNI, would fail to meet the European Council commitments on

---

[34] See European Commission, Communication on Enlargement Strategy and Main Challenges 2006–07, COM(2006) 649, Brussels, 8 November 2006(b), p. 20.

[35] See European Commission, Communication on the Financial Perspective 2007–13, COM(2004) 487, Brussels, 14 July 2004(b), pp. 3–4.

[36] See European Council, Presidency Conclusions of the Brussels European Council of 24-25 October, 14702/02, Brussels, 26 November 2002.

agricultural payments, would undermine the phasing-in of cohesion policy in the 10 new member states, and would jeopardise the existing levels in other policies, let alone to implement the new priorities".[37] According to the Commission, under such a scenario, the EU would for example (among other things) have to decrease cohesion support drastically in the old member states in the face of major problems of lagging development, unemployment and social exclusion.

The fact is that the own resources ceiling has been precisely set at around 1% of GNI, with a consequent cut of about €140 billion (or -14%) compared with the Commission's proposal (excluding the European development fund). Such a reduction can only reinforce the need for clarity about the relation between the objectives pursued and the outcomes expected. This point is notably true for the sectors having suffered the most from the Council's axe, such as competitiveness (-44%), citizenship, freedom, security and justice (-42%) and the EU as a global player (-31%).

The question is namely this: What are the consequences in terms of effectiveness of a financial framework that is quantitatively the same as for the 2000–06 period, despite 12 further member states and 110 million more inhabitants (moreover, with a lower income level)? One could wonder in particular whether, as a result of these cuts, the objectives have been reviewed and more selectivity has been introduced in the programmes or whether the Commission had been simply too generous in its forecast.

The Commission has emphasised that despite the constraints in financial resources, a comparison with the previous 2000–06 financial framework would show a 69% increase in the areas of competitiveness for growth and employment[38] and a 21% increase for cohesion for growth and

---

[37] See European Commission (2004a), pp. 26–27.

[38] See European Commission, "Q&A on Interinstitutional Agreement on Budgetary Discipline and Sound Financial Management 2007-2013", Memo 06/204, Brussels, 17 May 2006(j).

The rise would be seen in the following areas:

- 139% increase for transport and energy,
- 81% increase for environment-friendly transport (Marco Polo II),
- 75% increase for research (7th Research Framework Programme),
- 60% increase for the Competitiveness and Innovation Programme, and

employment,[39] whilst citizenship, freedom, security and justice recorded a spectacular increase (+78%). Nevertheless, these are limited shifts, especially to finance policies in the framework of the Lisbon strategy,[40] which were largely included in the previous internal policies. Out of the 59 programmed actions planned, only a couple can actually be considered really new initiatives. In this regard, the Sapir report stressed that "there is considerable inertia in the allocation of EU spending and the choice of spending priorities does not square with the Union's present economic priorities," and this "allows for only minor tinkering".[41]

Since total revenue is strictly limited by the own resources ceiling, once administrative expenditure is accounted for, the other policies must share for the seven-year period the around €135 billion slice of the cake left by the two big spending areas. This portion is no more than 0.16% of the EU GNI, or 16% of the commitment appropriations available.

One would expect that if, for whatever reason, the financial resources are limited, the targets should be set accordingly and at a level permitting

---

- 52% increase for knowledge/training (Lifelong Learning and Erasmus Mundus Programmes).

[39] Ibid. More specifically, the growth would be seen in these areas:
- 11% increase for structural policies, and
- 74% increase for the cohesion fund.

[40] For a definition, see footnote 7.

[41] See Sapir et al. (2003), pp. 126 and 162. That is not to say, however, that nothing has changed. For example, in the research area, a strong focus has been put on major research themes within the largest programme component of FP7 – Cooperation – to make the programme more flexible and responsive to the needs of industry. FP7 is also establishing new regions of knowledge that bring together the various research partners within a region. A new funding instrument, the Joint Technology Initiatives, specifically addresses those areas of research activity where enhanced collaboration and considerable investment are essential to long-term success. A specific programme (Ideas) will support 'frontier research' on the sole basis of scientific excellence, in any area of science or technology and without obligation for cross-border partnerships. The European Research Council (ERC) will oversee the funding of this programme, which entails appropriations for about 15% of the whole FP7. ERC is the first pan-European funding body set up to support investigator-driven frontier research. The ERC complements other funding activities in Europe such as those of the national research funding agencies.

the achievement of a critical and perceivable scale of action. Indeed, with the aim of ensuring that the objectives are met, one of the guiding principles of the Commission's financial perspective proposal was to concentrate the Community resources on a few major initiatives. This was because "sound financial planning means matching resources to needs. As financial resources are limited, financial decisions are essentially about choices to be made and priorities to be fixed."[42]

Looking purely at the volume of funds allocated to the programmes, only 9 out of the 59 programmes record appropriations of more than €1 billion per year. As is shown in Table 1.2, the four biggest programmes, accounting for a large share of the financial perspective (77%), are unsurprisingly concentrated in structural or agricultural policies. It should also be noted that there is no large programme under the citizenship, freedom, security and justice heading. In this respect, the European Parliament has observed that the relevance of this heading, although still acceptable in political terms, "may be questioned in terms of the volume of appropriations compared with all the other headings".[43]

---

[42] See European Commission (2004a), p. 26. In this respect, the Agenda 2000 programme underlined 10 years ago that "the relevance of policies, structures and procedures should be examined critically in a screening process preceding decisions on funding programmes and allocating resources to their management". It also stressed that "[c]onsideration should be given to the appropriate size of programmes and projects supported financially by the Community to ensure that the programmes deliver a clear added value at European level". It acknowledged, because of budgetary constraints, a need "to identify more clearly the core functions on which the Commission should concentrate" (see European Commission, *Agenda 2000, Communication for a Stronger and Wider Union*, Vol. I, 97/6, Brussels, 15 June 1997(a), pp. 47–48). Agenda 2000 was meant to respond to the 'threats' of globalisation and a multi-polar world. It outlined a large spectrum of actions, from institutional reform (the weighting of votes in the Council and a reduction in the size of the Commission) to policy reforms, such as continuing to reform the CAP (to take further the movement towards world market prices coupled to direct income aids), pursuing the priority goal of economic and social cohesion (to foster competitive development and lasting growth to create jobs throughout the Union), strengthening internal policies (to promote a high quality of life, a sound environment, freedom, security and justice), enhancing the pre-accession aid to applicant countries and absorbing the impact of the first enlargement. See also the section "The 'European' added value: What is it?".

[43] See European Parliament, Resolution of 8 June 2005 (op. cit.), para. 36.

Table 1.2 Financial perspective 2007–13 – The most important spending programmes (€ million, commitment appropriations, current prices)

Headings	Total	% of Financial perspective	% of Heading/ subheading	Average/ year
Sustainable growth	409,961	42.06	95.14	58,566
Competitiveness for growth and employment	62,551	6.42	74.82	8,936
1. Research Framework Programme	54,538	5.59	65.24	7,791
2. Trans-European Transport Network	8,013	0.82	9.58	1,145
Cohesion for growth and employment	347,410	35.64	100.00	49,630
3. Structural funds	277,703	28.49	79.94	39,672
4. Cohesion fund	69,707	7.15	20.06	9,958
Preservation & management of natural resources	407,477	41.80	97.30	58,211
5. Agricultural market expenditure and direct aids	318,988	32.72	76.17	45,570
6. Rural development	88,489	9.08	21.13	12,641
The EU as a global player	39,656	4.07	71.07	5,665
7. Development cooperation Instrument	16,958	1.74	30.39	2,423
8. Instrument for Pre-Accession	11,476	1.18	20.57	1,639
9. European Neighbourhood and Partnership Instrument	11,222	1.15	20.11	1,603
Total	857,094	87.93	–	–

Source: Own calculations based on the European Commission's (2007j) Financial Programming 2007–13.

Table 1.3 Financial perspective 2007–13 – Medium-size spending programmes (€ million, commitment appropriations, current prices)

Headings	Total	% of Financial perspective	% of Heading/ subheading	Average/ year
Sustainable growth	11,596	1.19	2.69	1,657
Competitiveness for growth and employment	11,596	1.19	13.87	1,657
1. Lifelong learning	6,970	0.72	8.34	996
2. Competitiveness and Innovation Framework Programme	3,621	0.37	4.33	517
3. Galileo	1,005	0.10	1.20	144
Preservation & management of natural resources	8,849	0.91	2.11	1,264
4. European fisheries fund	4,340	0.45	1.04	620
5. Common fisheries policy and Law of the Sea	2,412	0.25	0.58	345
6. Life+	2,098	0.22	0.50	300
Citizenship, freedom, security and justice	1,820	0.19	14.92	260
Freedom, security and justice	1,820	0.19	24.59	260
7. External borders fund	1,820	0.19	24.59	260
The EU as a global player	13,904	1.43	24.92	1,986
8. Humanitarian aid	5,614	0.58	10.06	802
9. Instrument for Stability	2,062	0.21	3.70	295
10. Common foreign and security policy	1,981	0.20	3.55	283
11. Emergency aid reserve	1,744	0.18	3.13	249
12. Loan guarantee reserve	1,400	0.14	2.51	200
13. European Instrument for Democracy and Human Rights	1,104	0.11	1.98	158
Total	36,169	3.71	–	–

Source: Own calculations based on the European Commission's (2007j), Financial Programming 2007–13.

Most of the 50 remaining programmes have been granted appropriations of less than €1 billion for the whole 2007–13 period (inter alia, all programmes devoted to the citizenship subheading). In fact, 27 of them are worth less than €0.5 billion, and a full 20 of those programmes have funding of less than €0.2 billion.

Table 1.3 above presents the 13 programmes worth at least €1 billion. These are mainly concentrated on external actions: only two among them (lifelong learning and humanitarian aid) represent appropriations accounting for more than 0.5% of the total financial perspective. Under the citizenship, freedom, security and justice heading, the external borders fund is actually the largest programme in absolute terms for the whole heading (it also represents one-fourth of the total subheading appropriations).

The combination of a limited amount of appropriations available as a whole and the retention of existing programmes has resulted in a reduced budget for most of these initiatives. Irrespective of the interest and the qualities of the individual programmes, one may ask whether the volume of the appropriations for many of the programmes is enough to make the EU's actions in these domains meaningful and visible across the 27 member states. More specifically, the issue is whether it is possible to achieve critical masses of material, human and intellectual resources to respond to the generally very ambitious objectives. The risk is, for some of these actions at least, that they will be no more than symbolic and will merely 'mark the territory' of the EU budget.

One example is given by the programmes under the competitiveness for growth and employment subheading, at the heart of the Lisbon strategy. These programmes are meant to support the Union's physical and knowledge infrastructure. Despite a cut in the appropriations available well above 40%,[44] this subheading still encompasses expenditure on a wide

---

[44] The Commission's financial perspective proposal entailed appropriations amounting to €132.8 billion (2004 prices). This amount has been reduced to €74.1 billion in the financial perspective. For example, in the field of the trans-European networks (TENs) for transport and energy, the amounts finally decided (€8.2 billion) were significantly lower than the budgetary resources set out in the Commission's proposal (€20.7 billion), although representing a doubling of the resources for the transport projects (benefiting from the overwhelming share of the resources) as compared with the 2000–06 period. In this respect, the European Parliament remarked that "selecting and prioritising projects will become even

range of actions (research and innovation, education and training, security and environmental sustainability of EU networks, support for an integrated single market and the accompanying policies, and implementation of the social policy agenda).

When looking at the present 16 actions planned under the competitiveness for growth and employment subheading and worth less than €1 billion per year, the three largest programmes (the Lifelong Learning Programme, the Competitiveness and Innovation Framework Programme and Galileo) represent altogether no more than 1.2% of the financial perspective. The other 13 programmes have to share among them an amount of €3.15 billion, hence the average value of these programmes is no more than €0.242 billion for the whole period. In comparison, the average value of programmes worth less than €1 billion under the headings of freedom, security, justice, and citizenship and the EU as a global player range from €0.349 billion to €0.416 billion. The European Parliament has expressed concern "that previous innovation and competitiveness programmes have failed to deliver the necessary link between fundamental and applied research and industrial innovation partly due to the fact that the financial resources were rather limited".[45]

The EU's satellite navigation system Galileo is one of the programmes under the competitiveness subheading. The High-Level Group on the trans-European transport network viewed the project as being of particularly important strategic interest as it is meant to provide the EU with an autonomous radio navigation system, thus improving efficiency and safety in all transport modes while at the same time guaranteeing the EU's technological independence in this area.[46] Owing to the failed

---

more important" because of the reduction of appropriations compared with the initial Commission proposal and thus Parliament asked the Commission "to set up a comprehensive list of clear criteria which allow projects to be prioritised in a transparent manner" (see European Parliament, Resolution of 24 April 2007 on the discharge for implementation of the European Union general budget for the financial year 2005, paras 194 and 199).

[45] See European Parliament, Resolution of 8 June 2005 (op. cit.), para. 52.

[46] The High-Level Group, chaired by Karel Van Miert, was mandated by the Commission to identify the priority projects of the trans-European transport network up to 2020 on the basis of proposals from the member states and the acceding countries. The Group delivered its report on 27.6.2003.

negotiations with the private consortium, which had initially been expected to secure at least two-thirds of the financing for the deployment phase, the Council decided in June 2007 that this phase would be funded with public money. [47] Thus, a further €2.4 billion is necessary over the next five years (2008–12), in addition to the €1 billion already foreseen in the financial perspective. Where this extra funding should come from has still to be decided. Two major funding options are theoretically available, i.e. funding by member states' contributions from outside the EU budget, for example through the European Space Agency (but 10 member states are not members of the ESA) or a revision of the financial perspective (favoured by the European Parliament). [48] Being aware that most member states are hostile to a review of the upper limits of the financial perspective,[49] the Commission has adopted a proposal of revision of the financial perspective 2007–13 without increasing the overall budgetary ceiling. Funding was found in the margins of different headings available in 2007 and in 2008 (mostly under heading 2, "Preservation & Management of Natural Resources"), money that otherwise will not be used and ought normally to reduce member states' contributions. [50] For this reason, several member

---

[47] See Council Resolution 10126/07 of 1 June 2007. See also European Commission, Communication on Galileo at a cross-road: The implementation of the European GNSS programmes, COM(2007) 261 final, Brussels, 16 May 2007(k) and the attached Working Document.

[48] See European Parliament, Resolution of 20 June 2007 on the financing of the European programme of satellite radio navigation (Galileo), para 8. An analysis of the various financing options has been provided by the Commission in its Communication on Progressing Galileo: The Re-Profiling of the European GNSS Programmes, COM(2007) 534, Brussels, 19 September 2007(n).

[49] By launching the development phase of the Galileo project, the Council decided in 2002 "that member states will not be requested to make direct financial contributions of their own national resources to the GALILEO programme; any further public sector funding of GALILEO, in any of its phases, should be met by redeployment under the appropriate ceilings of the Financial Perspectives in force at that time" (see European Transport and Telecommunications Council, Conclusions of the 2420th Council meeting, 7282/02, Brussels, 25–26 March 2002, pp. 20-21).

[50] See European Commission, Communication Concerning the Revision of the Multi-annual Financial Framework (2007–13), COM(2007) 549, Brussels, 19 September 2007(o). Since the amount at stake for the revision is below 0.03% of the EU GNI within the margin for unforeseen expenditure, the decision to revise the

states might favour instead a redeployment of funds within the competitiveness subheading and hence an across-the-board reduction for several programmes (namely research, lifelong learning and Erasmus). The Commission observed, however, that these programmes have all been adopted with their respective envelopes and claimed therefore that at this stage significant changes are not possible, except for the €300 million available within the transport-related research programmes dedicated to Galileo under the 7th Research Framework Programme.

The proposed doubling of the EU's research funding (to an average of €10 billion per year) was justified by a full exploitation of the European added value of EU action (e.g. the growing pressure of international competition). More precisely, the substantial increase proposed by the Commission was meant to be crucial in restructuring research in the EU, in pooling and leveraging resources more widely, and in moving Europe closer to a real 'single market' for research.[51] The financial perspective has reduced the proposed amount to around €8 billion per year, however. This reduction has a consequence on meeting the Lisbon agenda goal of raising overall research investment in the EU from 1.9% of GDP to around 3% by 2010. This objective is based on the assumption that 1% will come from public sources and 2% from the private sector. The Commission has estimated that public investment in research in the member states is planned to increase to 0.88% of GDP by 2010, still below the 1% agreed target for the public spending share of the 3% Lisbon target.[52] It is therefore assumed that there is a gap of 0.12% of GDP. The EU research budget has actually been increased from 0.04% to 0.06% of EU GDP. This means that even though it represents almost 6% of the financial perspective (and the fifth largest spending area), the EU research budget can only cover half of the gap in the 1% target for public investment.

---

financial perspective can be adopted by a qualified majority in the Council and a majority of the members of the European Parliament with three-fifths of the votes cast. See also Box 1.1.

[51] See European Commission, *Impact assessment and* ex ante *evaluation of the 7th Framework Programme*, Annex 1, SEC(2005) 430, Brussels, 6 April 2005(b), p. 46.

[52] In its proposal for the financial perspective, the Commission made a strong case for a significant increase in EU research funding, as a contribution to bridging the remaining gap towards the 1% target of public investment. See European Commission (2004a), pp. 8–9 and 28.

A further example is provided by the structural policies, which, although accounting for about one-third of the EU budget, still represent a limited fraction of national investments in regional and social policies. Despite the increased disparities among the regions following the recent enlargements, all EU regions remain eligible for one or the other of the structural policy objectives, with a consequent drop in the aid per head of population.[53] Although approximately half of cohesion spending is intended for the new member states, there is still a concrete risk of fragmentation of the interventions. For example, the structural fund rules provide that EU-15 member states concentrate their co-financed investments towards the Lisbon objectives. At the same time, the regulation leaves them the choice among a large range of 47 types of actions within 9 priority themes, so it is hard to see a decisive attempt at selectivity.[54] The idea that all kinds of expenditures contribute effectively to the strategy is hardly credible. Moreover, these actions, which are not dissimilar to the interventions financed in past periods, risk overlapping with other programmes.

---

[53] According to a study made for the European Parliament, there will be a drop in funds per head of population in the convergence regions from approximately €3,134 per head of population (2000–06 period) to €2,501 in the 2007–13 period. The estimate has been made in constant 2004 euros, and according to the forecasts of the December 2005 Council. See European Parliament, *Measurement of impact of structural actions on employment, quality of life and infrastructure: Relevant indicators*, April 2006, p. 18. See also footnote 96.

[54] The priority themes are research and technological development, innovation and entrepreneurship; information society; transport; energy; environmental protection and risk prevention; increasing the adaptability of workers and firms, enterprises and entrepreneurs; improving access to employment and sustainability; improving the social inclusion of less-favoured persons; and improving human capital. The number of 47 types of actions is applicable to the 'convergence' regions. In regional competitiveness and employment, the eligible actions have been reduced to 33, which is still not really "a limited number of policy priorities" as the Commission intended to promote. Concerning structural policies in general, there are indications of a reduction in the size of projects. A comparison between the last two programming periods (1994–99 and 2000–06) shows a significant reduction (more than 60%) in both the number and funding for the so-called 'major projects', probably as a result of the increased threshold (from €25 million for infrastructure and €15 million for productive investments to €50 million for all projects).

These examples also show that agreement on the financial perspective implies a compromise between sometimes conflicting interests, i.e. whether the appropriations should be redirected towards policies for promoting growth through increased investments in knowledge or, on the contrary, whether the EU budget should increase its redistributive function. This issue furthermore arises against a background of tension between net-payer countries (wishing to limit their contribution to the EU budget)[55] and net recipients, with the Eastern European countries seeking to claim concrete evidence of the solidarity, repeatedly affirmed in the accession process, with their economically weak situations. But there are also different budget priorities put forward by different 'sponsors' (the Commission, the European Parliament, individual member states and, last but not least, the over 15,000 interest groups and lobbyists[56] with entrenched interests in EU spending). Which kinds of policies the EU should finance is, ultimately, not a harmless issue.

The final compromise is therefore a mixture of allocative, redistributive and stabilising measures in a context where the unanimous agreement of the member states is required. Indeed, reaching an agreement is a lengthy enterprise each time. It took almost two years to agree on the current 2007–13 financial perspective: four different presidencies of the Council dealt with this sensitive issue.[57] A flavour of this is given by the Council document containing the last (and finally adopted) proposal. The document states that the proposal consists of three parts (expenditure, revenue and review) considered "complementary and inseparable. This

---

[55] For example, in December 2003, when the Commission was about to present its proposal for a new 2007–13 financial perspective, six member states (France, Germany, Sweden, the Netherlands, Austria and the UK) made known their desire to see the ceiling for own resources reduced to "1.0% of GNI, including agriculture spending within the ceiling set by the European Council in October 2002". This issue is a recurrent one. In the minutes of the European Council meeting in Cardiff (see the Presidency Conclusions of the Cardiff European Council of 15-16 June, SN150/1/98 REV 1, Brussels, June 1998, para. 54) one could read, concerning the preparation of the 2000–06 financial perspective: "The European Council notes the Commission's working assumption that the existing Own Resources ceiling will be maintained, but that some member states have not accepted this."

[56] This is an estimate of Agence Europe, see the edition of 13 March 2007.

[57] The EC Treaty (Art. 203) provides that the office of president of the Council shall be held in turn by each member state for a term of six months.

means that the principle of nothing is agreed until everything is agreed continues to apply."[58]

Concluding remarks

The limitation on the financial resources made available to the EU budget requires increased selectivity in identifying the programmes to be financed. The simultaneous concentration on two main policies and the financing of a plurality of programmes runs the risk of ineffective spending, in particular through the dispersion of the financial resources. In order for EU spending to achieve perceivable effects, it seems necessary to concentrate the resources on priority actions, starting from a transparent scrutiny process of the present programmes.

The 'European' added value: What is it?

The *raison d'être* of the EU budget (and of the Commission's management powers in respect of it) lies in Art. 5 TEC, on the ground that "the objectives of the proposed action cannot be sufficiently achieved by the member states and can therefore, by reason of the scale or effects of the proposed action, be better achieved by the Community". In practice, this means that the EU budget should do things that nobody else can (or will) do with better results. Moreover, as most (if not all) member states are reluctant to see any significant increase in total public expenditure at both national and European levels, any increase of the EU budget should be offset by a corresponding reduction in the national budgets. In other words, where, between the EU budget and the national budgets, could the taxpayer's money be better invested?

Evidence about the European added value of EU expenditure is therefore crucial in convincing people that "the scale or effects of the proposed action cannot be sufficiently achieved by the member states" and that management at the EU level would be the most cost-effective method of achieving the objectives.[59] 'Convincing' is actually not an issue solely for the government representatives in charge of negotiating a financial perspective The EU budget matters to all citizens, both as taxpayers and as potential beneficiaries of the expenditure that they themselves pay for.

---

[58] See European Council (2005a), p. 1.

[59] For a critical analysis of the concept of European added value and its use in various policy settings, see Tarschys (2005).

Box 1.2 European added value and subsidiarity

The Commission has acknowledged on several occasions that the Community should be made responsible solely for those tasks that can be best carried out at the Community rather than the national level or for those tasks that, for other reasons, determine the progress towards integration. For example, the then President of the European Commission, Jacques Santer said in his investiture speech of 17 January 1995 before the European Parliament: "[W]e must make a constant effort to concentrate on essentials, to do at Community level only that which cannot be done at national level, in short to apply the principle of subsidiarity" (Santer, 1995). His successor, Romano Prodi, also recommended enabling "the Commission to deliver on our core business commitments in the years to come", in order to allow it to concentrate "on its real job and [do] it efficiently and well" (Prodi, 2000a). It is worth noting that the Commission tried, in 1978, to determine what the EU should be doing by identifying some criteria, such as "economies of scale", the "need of a comprehensive approach with other EU financed policies" or of "lightening the burden on national budgets". These criteria, however, were too vague to be made operational (European Commission, 1978, pp. 6–8). The European Convention has examined the issue of subsidiarity and concluded that this principle was essentially political in nature. Its implementation involved a considerable margin of discretion for the institutions (considering whether shared objectives could better be achieved at the European level or at another level). The monitoring of compliance with that principle should take place before the entry into force of the act in question. Also, *ex ante* political monitoring of the principle of subsidiarity should primarily involve national parliaments.* The European Parliament has observed that all expenditure from the EU budget should be designed to add European value to the public expenditure of member states, and that the principle of subsidiarity should be strictly respected with regard to spending decisions in the field of non-exclusive competence – in particular the criterion that EU action does, by reason of its scale or effects, better achieve the objectives of the Union.**

---

* See European Convention, Conclusions of the Working Group I on the Principle of Subsidiarity, CONV 286/02, Brussels, 23 September 2002.

** See European Parliament, Resolution of 8 June 2005 on Policy Challenges and Budgetary Means of the Enlarged Union 2007–13, para. 1.

Moreover, the perception of added value in EU expenditure also plays a role in determining citizens' attitudes towards Europe in general. Already in 1978, at a time when the EU budget represented no more than 10% of today's volume, the Commission observed, "As long as people believe that Community budgetary expenditure is an additional call on the national purse, their reaction will be to systematically curb such expenditure."[60] The proposed 2007–13 financial perspective provided the opportunity for the Commission to reaffirm the necessity "of a clear vision of what we want to do", in order "to maximise the impact of our common policies so that we further enhance the added value of every euro spent at European level".[61] This aspiration was set out with a view to "higher financial transparency, scope for improved quality and effectiveness of expenditure [and the] possibility to better assess Community value added".[62] One of the key assumptions for asking for a substantial increase of the appropriations in the 2007–13 period was precisely that "pooling national resources at EU level can bring major savings for national budgets" and that therefore "one euro spent at EU level can offer more than one euro at national level".[63]

This issue is actually the key one at the heart of the subsidiarity principle. It is nevertheless not sufficient to proclaim such added value – at the least, some degree of precision about the concrete achievements pursued should be provided. Indeed, effective results are not the inevitable consequence of the origin of the funds (the EU budget), nor are they a matter of idealism; they are rather the outcome of well-managed policies, with clear and achievable objectives, and defined expected results. The problem is that EU policies pursue a multiplicity of different targets,[64] with the risk of separated vertical strategies and limited or no synergies among the various strands and, not least, with the difficulty of drawing

---

[60] See European Commission (1978), p. 7.

[61] See European Commission (2004a), p. 4.

[62] Ibid., p. 30.

[63] See European Commission (2004b), pp. 5 and 8. See also the section "Financial perspective: Whose perspective?".

[64] The Sapir report observed that "quite often in the EU economic system, policy instruments are assigned two objectives at the same time: for example, fostering growth and improving cohesion. It would be better to assign one objective to each policy instrument." See Sapir et al. (2003), p. 4.

crosscutting conclusions. For example, the Lisbon strategy,[65] at the heart of the financial perspective, is implemented through a number of different programmes, each of them dealing with multiple (although connected) objectives. This approach raises the issue of how coordination and added value will be achieved in substantive terms.[66]

Structural policies are one of the main items of the Lisbon agenda.[67] In the impact analysis prepared by the Commission for the present programming period, a specific section is dedicated to the Community added value.[68] The document is rather convincing in stating that EU

---

[65] A definition of the Lisbon strategy is given in footnote 7.

[66] For example, to the question "Has real change been achieved in policies addressing social inclusion?" the evaluation report of the EU programme to promote member state cooperation to combat social exclusion and poverty states: "Real change so far has probably only been achieved in a small number of cases, where all the conditions were right for learning and implementation." The overall conclusion is that the programme has made a good contribution at the strategic level. Nevertheless, the programme could "have achieved more through greater focus and coherence, involving more active, ongoing management of thematic integration between the actions at both EU and national levels" (see European Commission, *Evaluation of the EU programme to promote member state co-operation to combat social exclusion and poverty*, Main Report, December 2006(c), pp. 74–75).

[67] In financial terms, the most important programmes contributing to the Lisbon strategy are the structural policies and the 7th Research and Development Framework Programme (FP7). For structural policies, the EU-15 member states are to ensure that 60% of expenditure on the convergence objective and 75% of expenditures on the regional competitiveness and employment objective target the EU priorities of promoting competitiveness and creating jobs, including meeting the objectives of the Integrated Guidelines for Growth and Jobs (see Council Regulation (EC) No. 1083/2006 of 11 July 2006, laying down general provisions on the European Regional Development Fund, the European Social Fund and the Cohesion Fund and repealing Regulation (EC) No. 1260/1999, OJ L 210, 31.7.2006, Art. 9(3)). It is nonetheless likely that an important part of the operations co-financed in the other member states will also focus on the Lisbon objectives. Preliminary Commission estimates suggest that, overall, the member states have earmarked for Lisbon investments around €200 billion. Almost €50 billion or 15% of the overall cohesion budget will be allocated to research and innovation, about equal to the total of the 7th Framework Programme for Research.

[68] See the European Commission's *Proposal of a legislative package revising the regulations applicable to the management of the Structural and of Cohesion Funds:*

cohesion policy has contributed (and will contribute) to inducing changes in the member states' policies, enhancing principles such as programming and strategic approach, multilevel governance and evaluation.[69] Yet, the link between these expected 'qualitative' impacts and the level of EU expenditure is not made explicit. The document basically takes the view of typological continuity in the interventions between the previous (2000–06) period and the new programming periods. It also assumes a linear progressivity of the impacts, as it simply extrapolates to the new programming period estimated impacts from the previous period. In this way, it concluded that EU funds in the regional competitiveness and employment regions would create one-third of the new jobs necessary to reach the 70% employment rate by 2010 as fixed by the Lisbon strategy. The document admits that the low level of funding does not permit a credible evaluation of the effect on the GDP. It nevertheless provides, for the convergence regions, growth simulations on GDP, employment, investment and productivity based on a macroeconomic model, which, according to the Court of Auditors' examination of *ex post* evaluations, "suffered from significant limitations".[70]

A comprehensive impact analysis is of the outmost importance in the case of structural policies where there is no definite link between the funds allocated to a given region and the identification of intervention priorities, the ability to put forward suitable projects and the capacity to handle the interventions (during and after implementation).[71] This would seem a pre-condition of the Commission's ambition to retain "the political duty to define the strategic objectives and the frameworks of expenditure

---

Analysis of impact in the enlarged Union, Commission Working Paper, SEC(2004) 924, Brussels, 14 July 2004(c).

[69] Danuta Hübner, the European Commissioner responsible for Regional Policy, has defined cohesion policy as a "Trojan horse" to improve and modernise public administrations, to enhance transparency and to foster good governance (Hübner, 2007, p. 3).

[70] The Court referred to the Hermin model. See European Court of Auditors, *Special Report No. 10/2006 on* ex post *evaluations of Objectives 1 and 3 programmes 1994 to 1999,* OJ C 302, 12.12.2006(a), pp. 4 and 23.

[71] Concerning the difficulties of executing the forecasted expenditure, see the section "Is the size of the budget a major issue?".

programmes".[72] With an eye to the future, policy-makers would have been interested in knowing more about the expected results of the various operations financed for each region/country under the EU cohesion policy objective of "reducing disparities between the levels of development of the various regions".[73] One could recall in this respect that following concerns expressed in the Maastricht Treaty about "the need to monitor regularly the progress made towards achieving economic and social cohesion",[74] the Council ensured that in the future "assistance will be allocated where appraisal shows medium term economic and social benefits commensurate with the resources deployed. Operations should be adjusted to accord with the results of monitoring and evaluation."[75] Actually, the Constitutional Treaty repeated the same concerns expressed in 1992.[76]

Concerning research expenditure, another important item of the Lisbon agenda, an expert panel had concluded that it was necessary for the Commission to take "a leading role in developing a simple and robust definition of European Added Value taking into account the latest research on the need for government intervention and the need to develop lead

---

[72] See European Commission (2004a), p. 32.

[73] See Art. 158 TEC. The European Parliament has observed that "there is a lack of detailed information and comparative studies with rankings on the advancement of regions that profit from Structural Funds" and "the fact that funding has been granted does not guarantee per se that it will be put to good use" (see European Parliament, Resolution of 12 July 2007 on the role and effectiveness of cohesion policy in reducing disparities in the poorest regions of the EU, points H and P). The Commission's fourth cohesion report provides an outlook with regard to economic, social and territorial cohesion and also attempts to analyse, although indirectly, the impact of cohesion policy at the national and Community levels, particularly in terms of the structure of spending (see European Commission, *Growing Regions, Growing Europe, Fourth Report on Economic and Social Cohesion*, Official Publications of the European Communities, Luxembourg, May 2007(p)).

[74] See the Protocol on Economic and Social Cohesion attached to the Maastricht Treaty of 1992.

[75] See European Council, Presidency Conclusions of the European Council in Edinburgh, 11-12 December 1992.

[76] See para. 7 of the Protocol on Economic, Social and Territorial Cohesion attached to the Treaty establishing a Constitution for Europe of 2004.

markets for European solutions".[77] In this respect it is to be welcomed that, for the first time, the 2007–13 Framework Programme proposals have been accompanied by an *ex ante* impact assessment, based on an econometric model, with the aim of restricting the programme to actions "with a clear European value added" in order "to maximise positive impacts".[78] The impact assessment contains a specific section dedicated to the European added value of Community intervention that, while admitting that European added value is a complex concept, provides a clear analysis of the objectives and the reasons for EU intervention in research. Indeed, in general, EU-funded research has high added value by encouraging researchers to cooperate across national boundaries and to share complementary skills and knowledge, thus generating in particular a 'behavioural additionality' favouring continuation of collaborative research in the future. Intervention at the EU level promotes competition in research, leading to higher quality and excellence. In addition, EU-funded research may make possible projects that, because of their complexity and large scale, go beyond what is possible at the national level. Finally, EU research provides a framework for disseminating research results across Europe.

The document is very much focused on the likely impact of research expenditure in general. It could have been useful to examine to what extent this (moreover increased) EU research funding will help to achieve the Lisbon target of reaching expenditure equal to 3% of GDP by 2010. Indeed, this target is for Europe as a whole, not for individual member states, which have a variable level of R&D spending, some member states being in this respect leading or at least average performers, while others are catching up or even losing ground.[79] The issue is even more important as it

---

[77] See European Commission, *Five-Year Assessment of the European Union Research Framework Programmes 1999–2003*, Brussels, December 2004(d), p. 8.

[78] See European Commission (2005b), Main report, p. 12. The first research framework programme was launched in 1984.

[79] For example, Sweden and Finland spend on R&D more than 3% of their GDP. Denmark, Germany, Austria and France are spending more than the EU average of 1.93%. Other member states vary from the Netherlands and the UK, which are only just under the EU average, to less than 0.4% of GDP in Latvia and Cyprus. Only 10 member states have fixed an R&D target for 2010 of at least 3%. A similar situation applies at the regional level. The European Commission's fourth progress report on cohesion reveals worrying disparities in modern infrastructure, research and

is admitted that some research areas are insufficiently covered by national spending, while a considerable overlap exists in other areas of national research.[80]

The European Commission's report, *Key Figures 2007 on Science, Technology and Innovation*, shows that EU R&D intensity (R&D expenditure as a percentage of GDP) has stagnated since the mid-1990s. In 2005, only 1.84% of GDP was spent on R&D in the EU-27 and it remains at a lower level than in the US, Japan or South Korea. The Commission has stressed that high R&D intensity can be achieved when high contributions from the private sector go hand in hand with high levels of public funding.[81] While the 3% Lisbon objective assumes that 2% will come from the private sector, more than 85% of the R&D intensity gap between the EU-27 and its main competitors is caused precisely by the low rate of the EU's business sector in EU spending.[82] This is because a considerable part of EU business research investment takes place in non-EU countries. Consequently, there is a net outflow of R&D funding from the EU to other countries (over €6 billion in 2001) as illustrated by Figure 1.4.[83] The situation is admittedly similar for the flow of researchers.

---

education. For example, in 47 out of 254 regions, there is hardly any R&D, with expenditure on R&D below 0.5% of GDP. Collectively, these 47 regions account for approximately 0.5% of total R&D expenditure in the EU-27 (their GDP share is 3.5%). See European Commission, Communication on the Growth and Jobs Strategy and the Reform of European cohesion policy: Fourth progress report on cohesion, COM(2006) 281 final, Brussels, 12 June 2006(d), p. 6.

[80] See European Commission, "Why Europe Needs Research Spending", Memo 05/199, Brussels, 9 June 2005(c), p. 4; and also European Commission (2005b), Annex 1, pp. 24 and 55.

[81] See European Commission, "Low business R&D a major threat to European knowledge-based economy", Press release, IP/07/790, Brussels, 11 June 2007(a).

[82] Over the past 10 years, the R&D financed by the business sector has remained at around 1% of GDP in the EU. According to the Commission, the low level of private R&D expenditure in Europe in comparison with the US is mostly owing to differences in industrial structure and to the smaller size of the high-tech industry in the EU. See European Commission (2007a).

[83] It should be noted that EU investment in the US even exceeded the flow of intra-EU member states' R&D investment in 2001 (€15,399 million versus €13,644 million). *Key Figures 2007 on Science, Technology and Innovation: Towards a European*

Figure 1.4 Attractiveness of the EU for R&D investments (in € million PPS 2001)

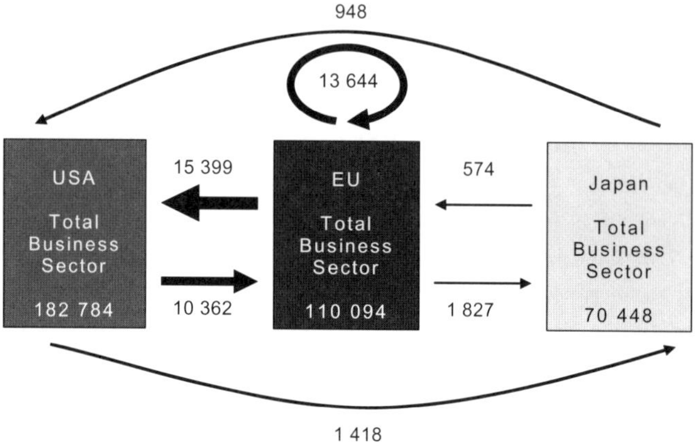

Source: European Commission (2005b), Annex 1, p. 16.

It seems clear that the whole process of linking funds, policies and objectives would benefit from increased transparency, an explicit 'intervention logic' describing how an intervention is expected to attain its global objectives.[84] In this respect, the cost of a policy is not just equal to the budgetary appropriations, as has indeed been observed:

Knowledge Area (European Commission, Brussels, 11 June 2007(b)) shows that in 2003, the balance of R&D investment flow between the US and EU-15 member states was negative for the latter by 4.4 billion of PPS (PPS is an artificial currency that reflects differences in national price levels that are not taken into account by exchange rates. This unit allows meaningful volume comparisons of economic indicators among countries).

[84] "Intervention logic" is "the conceptual link from an intervention's inputs to the production of its outputs and, subsequently, to its impacts on society in terms of results and outcomes" (see European Commission, *Evaluating EU activities – A Practical Guide for Commission Services*, Brussels, July 2004(e), p. 106). The European Parliament, while considering that "the Commission is the guardian of the Treaties and is responsible for defining the Community interest" has stressed the importance for the EU budget "to be established in accordance with the financial principles of the systematic sequence of the definition of tasks, the planning of expenditure, the securing of revenue and evaluation and that, when the tasks are defined, a distinction should be made between regulatory and fiscal tasks" (see European Parliament, Resolution of 11 March 1999, op. cit., paras 1 and 3).

Resources allocated in the budget for a given policy should also cover the 'delivery' costs of that policy, that is, the administrative costs of designing, implementing, monitoring and ex post evaluating any given policy. This should demonstrate which are cost-efficient policies and the good management practices. …Evaluation should also be applied to the financial and management practices according to criteria specified ex-ante. Monitoring and evaluation should allow the disbursement of EU money to be made conditional on its past efficient use.[85]

There is a need for a more focused *ex ante* role when approving the financial perspective and, later, the annual budget, especially with regard to the match between resources and measurable objectives, performance targets and indicators. Only if evaluation evidence related to past programmes is available can the budgetary authority exert any real influence in the budget decision-making.

In this context, the Court of Auditors' review of the *ex post* evaluation for the 1994–99 period for structural policies revealed a number of shortcomings in the approach and in the quality of the assessments made.[86] Notably, the objectives set lacked clarity and coherence, few performance indicators were available and an appropriate balance between quantitative and qualitative analysis was not always achieved. These weaknesses resulted in conclusions being drawn that were not supported by adequate analysis. The conclusions reached in a recent study ordered by the European Parliament were no less worrying.[87] The study concluded that there is a lack of a common methodology on impact evaluation that would allow a synthesis of the influence of the actions as a whole on a specific territory or region, and the particular added value for each fund and initiative. The monitoring and supervision system implemented prevented the results from being integrated with the actions and outcomes obtained in a given region. A direct link between actions and their impact on growth could not be established. The study also concluded that there is a lack of general criteria and common indicators for determining the impact of structural funds on other policies at the EU level and their synergies with other actions taken in eligible regions. The European Parliament has

---

[85] See Sapir et al. (2003), p. 165. A similar concern was raised in the framework of the initiatives to improve the Commission's management – see footnote 249.

[86] See European Court of Auditors (2006a).

[87] See European Parliament (2006), pp. 7–8.

recently invited the Commission "to demonstrate to what extent the methodology for ex ante, midterm and ex post evaluation has been consolidated" in order to prevent the errors of the past.[88]

It is to be welcomed that, for the first time in 2006, the Commission published a synthesis of policy achievements, which "sets out what the Commission has done to help realise its five-year strategic objectives".[89] Indeed, this is an impressive review of initiatives and legislative proposals that, however, does not yet say very much about the actual achievements of EU-funded policies. The same could be said of the recent Annual Evaluation Review.[90] The Review, which reports the results of completed evaluations, gives a generally positive conclusion about the relevance and the added value of the different EU policies. Yet, if one looks for example in the policy sections concerning structural policies, the information provided is rather limited and often concentrated on the kinds of actions that have been financed but not on their expected impact. It is therefore of limited value for preparing future activities, including, if need be, corrective actions.[91] As has been observed, there is a 'delivery deficit': "[T]he citizen is all too well aware of what is being spent through the EU budget, but very much less aware of what is being achieved as a result of that spending."[92]

---

[88] See European Parliament, Resolution of 24 April 2007 (op. cit.), para. 266.

[89] See European Commission, Communication on Policy Achievements in 2005, COM(2006) 124, Brussels, 14 March 2006(e), p. 2. For the year 2006, see European Commission, Communication on Policy Achievements in 2006, COM(2007) 67, Brussels, 28 February 2007(c). See also European Commission, Communication on the Synthesis of the Commission's Management Achievements in 2006, COM(2007) 274, Brussels, 30 May 2007(d).

[90] See European Commission, Communication on the Annual Evaluation Review 2006, COM(2007) 300, Brussels, May 2007(e).

[91] The section of the document dealing with "Preparing future activities" is limited for structural policies to elaborating a roadmap in the framework of "Gender equality".

[92] See European Convention, Contribution of Lord Tomlinson, "EU Budget: Building-in enhanced scrutiny of sound financial management", CONV 635/03, Brussels, 25 March 2003(a), pp. 2-3. It is worth noticing that one of the arguments invoked by the European Parliament for refusing to grant discharge to the Commission for the financial year 1996 (and which led to the resignation of the Santer Commission – see the section "The need for a management culture") was the lack of clarity as to whether the significant funds "made available in the

The European Parliament has stressed the link existing between the development of the financial resources allocated to the Union and their use "for actions with real European added value, clearly defined priorities and visibility for citizens",[93] to the point "that an initiative that is insufficiently verifiable should not be financed by public money".[94]

It must be recognised that assessing the relationship between EU-specific policies and particular effects is a difficult exercise. Indeed, the financial size of EU policies, although not insignificant in absolute terms, is relatively small. For example, national programmes still account for the vast bulk of public research spending in the EU.[95] The same is true for the structural policies,[96] although representing about one-third of the EU budget. That being said, one should not forget that the financial perspective is a rather rigid framework decided for seven years as a global package of multi-annual actions, often based on all-inclusive objectives. And 'absorption' of the funds is itself an implicit objective. If, because of

---

Community budget for a virtually unmanageable number of measures to promote small and medium-sized enterprises (SMEs)…will help to meet the aim of creating more jobs" and that "the Commission until now was totally unable to explain how this money has been allocated" (see European Parliament, Resolution of 31 March 1998 informing the Commission of the reasons for the postponement of the discharge in respect of the implementation of the general budget of the European Union for the 1996 financial year, paras 22–23).

[93] See European Parliament, Resolution of 8 June 2005 (op. cit.), para. 7.

[94] In this respect, the Parliament referred to the Court of Auditors' special reports on the European social fund combating early school leaving and on rural development (see European Parliament, Resolution of 24 April 2007, op. cit., paras 205 and 238).

[95] The 6th Research and Development Framework Programme represented 5–6% of total EU public R&D expenditure.

[96] A study commissioned by the European Parliament concluded for example that the volume of structural actions on employment is not sufficient to modify the structural or current performance of regional economies. It added that the European social fund is increasingly oriented towards supporting what are called "active employment strategies", through the European employment strategy, in particular improvements in human capital skills and training. But the impact of these actions on sustaining or even creating jobs cannot be clearly established. See European Parliament (2006), p. 8. See also footnote 53.

methodological weaknesses (for example, the lack of specific and measurable objectives) or simply owing to a reduced scale of funding, it is not possible to achieve (and identify) the desired results of the actions, the risk is that concerns about the maximum take-up of funding will take precedence over the implementation of a coherent strategy aiming at the efficient, effective and economic use of the expenditure. There would be pressure to execute the earmarked expenditure,[97] to the point that the spending rate could well become the main indicator of the implementation of programmes, thus basically equating the European value added to the EU budget contribution.

Considering that a high rate of expenditure is proof of the implementation of its budgetary priorities, the European Parliament is normally quite attentive to ensuring that the 'spending' objective materialises in practice. In a recent Resolution, the Parliament expressed concern at the renewed increase in outstanding commitments and called for a higher rate of utilisation over the next three years. In so doing, it pointed to the low payment implementation rate in several cases.[98]

Concluding remarks

Without indisputable evidence of their added value, as compared with similar national expenditures, it will not be possible to persuade policy actors that EU policies should be kept at their present level or should even be enhanced.

One might wonder whether, just as the Commission cannot make any proposal for a Community act "without providing the assurance that that proposal or that measure is capable of being financed within the limit of the Community's own resources",[99] it should equally provide an assurance as to the possibility of setting "specific, measurable, achievable, relevant and

---

[97] See in this respect the example referred to in footnote 297.

[98] For example, the Parliament viewed as being low the expenditure rate for transport safety (74%), the Marco Polo programme (53%), the Daphne programme (58%) and the area of freedom, security and justice (80%). See European Parliament, Resolution of 24 April 2007 (op. cit.), paras 9, 117, 132 and 136.

[99] See Art. 270 TEC. This provision was introduced by the Maastricht Treaty to ensure budgetary discipline.

timed objectives".[100] This assurance should be, in the full sense, one of the criteria enacted in Art. 5 TEC so that one could conclude whether the objectives of the action envisaged can "by reason of the scale or effects...be better achieved by the Community". In this way, it would be possible to enhance the role of the EU budget as an instrument of action and potential achievements, as opposed to pre-agreed intergovernmental redistribution.

---

[100] As prescribed by Art. 27 of the Financial Regulation No. 1605/2002 of 25 June 2002 (op. cit.),

> Specific, measurable, achievable, relevant and timed objectives shall be set for all sectors of activity covered by the budget. Achievement of those objectives shall be monitored by performance indicators for each activity and information shall be provided by the spending authorities to the budgetary authority. ...Institutions shall undertake both ex ante and ex post evaluations...which shall be applied to all programmes and activities [that] entail significant spending and evaluation results disseminated to spending, legislative and budgetary authorities.

See also footnote 289.

2. READS AS 'OWN RESOURCES', MEANS NATIONAL CONTRIBUTIONS

The EU budget is financed from three main sources of revenue. The first of these are *customs duties,* levied at the external frontiers of the EU, together with *agricultural levies,* in particular on the production and storage of sugar and isoglucose. The second source of revenue is represented by the *VAT own resource,* which is levied on member states' statistical 'notional' *harmonised* VAT bases, calculated on the basis of national VAT receipts. The third resource is a residual resource used to balance the budget. It is levied at a uniform rate in proportion to the GNI of each member state (Table 2.1).

Table 2.1 The composition of the EU's own resources 1996–2006 (% and € million, cash basis)

	Customs duties and agricultural levies (%)	VAT resource (%)	GNI resource (%)	Total (€ million)
1996	19	51	30	71,177
1997	19	45	36	75,415
1998	17	40	43	82,223
1999	17	38	45	82,700
2000	17	40	43	88,040
2001	18	39	43	80,788
2002	12	29	59	77,550
2003	13	26	61	83,352
2004	13	15	72	95,201
2005	14	16	70	100,942
2006	15	17	68	102,367

Source: European Commission (2007l).

Out of the taxpayer's sight, out of mind

Unlike the ECSC Treaty, which was financed through levies on the production of coal and steel paid directly by producing companies (hence by a real Community tax),[101] the EEC budget (like the Euratom budget) was initially financed by a system of member states' contributions.[102] Yet, the EEC Treaty of 1957 had foreseen the possibility of replacing national contributions by own resources.[103] In 1965, the Commission presented a global package of measures aimed at establishing a link between financing the CAP, raising independent revenue for the Community and wider budgetary powers for the European Parliament. Not only did the Commission propose a gradual transfer (as of July 1967) of the customs duties and agricultural levies to the EU budget, it also proposed amending Art. 201 of the EEC Treaty in order to allow the European Parliament (once

---

[101] See Art. 49 of the ECSC Treaty. This Treaty expired on 23 July 2002, under the terms of its Art. 97.

[102] Art. 200 of the founding Treaty establishing the European Economic Community (EEC Treaty) (1957) fixed as below the share of the financing among member states.

Table A. Financing share of the member states (%)

Member states	Administrative expenditure	Social fund
Belgium	7.9	8.8
Germany	28.0	32.0
France	28.0	32.0
Italy	28.0	20.0
Luxembourg	0.2	0.2
Netherlands	7.9	7.0
Total	100	100

Source: Art. 200, EEC Treaty.

Similarly, the Euratom Treaty established different scales of member states' contributions for the operating budget and the research and investment budget (Art. 172).

[103] See Art. 201 of the EEC Treaty. Art. 173 of the Euratom Treaty constituted an even more explicit move towards EU financial independence, as it provided that financial contributions could be replaced by the proceeds of levies collected by the Community in member states.

directly elected) to create independent sources of revenue for the Community. Thus, the member states' veto right would have disappeared.[104]

Although the Commission's proposals were not accepted in the end, concrete expectations were still raised by the European Council's Own Resources Decision of 1970.[105] This Decision established not only the principle that "the Communities shall be allocated resources of their own", but also that "from 1 January 1975 the budget of the Communities shall, irrespective of other revenue, be financed entirely from the Communities' own resources".[106] Since customs duties and agricultural levies were not sufficient to ensure the equilibrium of the budget, the Decision judged it advisable to allocate "to the Communities, in addition, tax revenue, the most appropriate being that accruing from the application of a single rate to the basis for assessing the value added tax, determined in a uniform manner for the member states".[107] The maximum call rate was set at 1% of the assessment base.

Actually, as explained in the following sections, the practice has evolved in such a way that the adjective 'own' before resources has become somewhat misleading, as it merely indicates the member states' obligation to finance the budget through national contributions, not the autonomy of

---

[104] See the Commission's proposals « Financement de la politique agricole commune - Ressources propres de la Communauté – Renforcement des pouvoirs du Parlement européen », COM(65) 150, Brussels, 31 March 1965.

[105] See Council Decision 70/243/ECSC, EEC, Euratom of 21 April 1970 on the replacement of financial contributions from member states by the Communities' own resources, OJ L 94, 28.4.1970. The role of the Own Resources Decision is described in footnote 9.

[106] Ibid., Arts 1 and 4.

[107] See the fifth successive para. introduced by "Whereas" and Art. 4 of Council Decision 70/243/ECSC, EEC, Euratom (op. cit.). Customs duties and agricultural levies were transferred to the Community in a gradual process lasting from 1971 to 1975, in order to mitigate the effects on the budgets of the member states. Because of a late introduction of the arrangements for a harmonised VAT base, member states continued to pay transitional national contributions replacing VAT resources until 1978 (this was done by six member states; three others – Germany, Ireland and Luxembourg – did so as of 1980 onwards).

the EU to fix and to manage its financial resources. Own resources are not to be equated with EU financial autonomy.[108]

There is an indirect link with the taxpayer for the so-called 'traditional own resources' (customs duties and agricultural levies).[109] Such a link does not exist at all for the GNI-based resource. The same applies to the VAT resource. Although potentially fulfilling the characteristic of "revenue accruing from other charges introduced within the framework of a

---

[108] The following definition of own resources is given by the Lamassoure report, a Working Document of the European Parliament on the European Communities' own resources:

> Own resources can be taken to mean a source of finance separate and independent of the member states, some kind of tax revenue assigned once and for all to the Community to fund its budget and due to it by right without the need for any subsequent decision by the national authorities. The member states, then, would be required to make payments available to the Community for its budget. (European Parliament, *Annexes to the Explanatory Statement, Working Document No. 1 on the European Communities Own Resources*, A6-0066/2007, 13 March 2007(a), p. 20)

A Commission document seems to claim that today the Communities' own resources already accrue to the EU budget "without the need for any subsequent decision by the national authorities" (see European Commission, *Updated check-list of administrative conditions in the area of the European Communities' own resources*, Brussels, November 2003(a), p. 5). This is actually a matter for interpretation. Member states may not indeed withhold at will their contributions to finance the budget (Art. 269 of the EC Treaty places on them a clear obligation in this respect); however, for an Own Resources Decision to enter into force a process of ratification in each member state according to their constitutional rules is required. For an analysis of the distinction between financial contributions and own resources, see Ehlermann (1982).

[109] An importer of goods from a third country is formally liable for any duties only vis-à-vis its national administration, and not the EU, although the latter is the 'institutional recipient' of this entitlement. The debtor vis-à-vis the EU is actually the member state where the import took place. Like GNI and VAT resources, traditional own resources are managed and collected by national administrations and subsequently made available to the Commission. The latter's role is limited to making sure that national systems operate in conformity with Community law. It should also be pointed out that any interest earned on traditional own resources prior to the amounts being made available to the Commission are owned by the member state involved, as well as penalties and late interest fees charged by the member states' authorities to the debtors.

common policy",[110] the VAT resource has simply been transformed in such a way as to produce a financial contribution, which is directly at odds with the initial objective.[111]

Concluding remarks

The expression 'own resources' suggests more than it actually means because the EU lacks genuine financial autonomy. As the Commission points out,

> The present financing system has ensured a smooth financing of the EU budget. However, in its present form the financing system lacks a direct link to citizens…The budgetary consequences of the Union's policies thus remain impalpable to the general public. With the overwhelming weight of the GNI resource, member states, and in particular net contributors, tend to judge EU policies and initiatives exclusively in terms of their national allocation and with little regard to the substance of policies, with the risk of obscuring the added value of EU policies.[112]

The VAT resource, voided of all substance

The introduction of a VAT-based resource was intended to achieve the overall objective of financing the EU budget entirely from own resources and to make available sufficient resources for its future development. Moreover, the VAT resource was also meant to be a Community tax, as the underlying assumption was to establish a link with the Community taxpayer.

The implementation of the VAT resource suffered initially from difficulties with establishing a common VAT system across the member

---

[110] This criterion was set by Council Decision 70/243/ECSC, EEC, Euratom of 21 April 1970 (op. cit.), Art. 2, to identify resources other than agricultural levies, sugar levies and customs duties. As a harmonised EU-wide tax, moreover with a very extensive assessment basis representing a large part of member states' income, VAT fulfils this requirement.

[111] See the following section and Box 2.1 in particular concerning the methods of calculation of the present VAT resource.

[112] See European Commission, *Financing the European Union, Commission report on the operation of the own resources system*, Vol. I, COM(2004) 505 final, Brussels, 14 July 2004(f), p. 8.

states and with defining the VAT assessment base.[113] Still, once it was operating 'at full capacity', the VAT resource began to fulfil its original function of becoming (at least potentially) the main own resource. It financed around half of the budget in 1981 and even more in the following years. To meet the costs of the enlargement to Spain and Portugal, the call rate was raised from 1% to 1.4% as of 1 January 1986, with the possibility of further increasing it to 1.6% as of 1 January 1988.[114]

The enlargement to Spain and Portugal coincided with a marked change in the destiny of this, until then, most promising EU resource. The VAT resource was increasingly accused of being inherently regressive on the ground that the VAT base is structurally higher in the least prosperous member states than it is in the richest ones.[115] This aspect of the matter was

---

[113] See footnote 107.

[114] See Council Decision 85/257/EEC, Euratom of 7 May 1985 on the Communities' system of own resources, OJ L 128, 14.5.1985, Art. 3(2) and the fourth successive para. introduced by "Whereas".

[115] Taxation in the form of VAT is generally considered regressive with relatively less well-off member states contributing proportionately more to the EU budget financing as a result of the lower share of savings in national income (the criterion of vertical equity is not satisfied – see European Commission, *Financing the European Union, Commission report on the operation of the own resources system*, COM(1998) 560, Brussels, 7 October 1998, annex 2, p. 8). The European Parliament highlighted in 1981 the necessity of ensuring greater equity among member states by introducing a corrective mechanism to VAT revenue (see European Parliament, Resolution of 9 April 1981 on the Community's own resources, paras 27-28). It emphasised this issue in 1990, noting "that VAT, which has become the main source of revenue, while having the advantage of being applied to a tax which is almost harmonized, has the grave disadvantage of interpersonal and spatial regressivity, and should therefore not occupy in future the pre-eminent position it enjoys at the moment" (see European Parliament, Resolution of 22 November 1990 on the future financing of the European Community, para. 16.). Yet some authors are not convinced that the regressivity of VAT is a real issue. For example, Begg, Grimwade & Price (1997), and Gretschmann (1998) challenge the opinion that the VAT resource has a significant regressive effect. The regressivity of the VAT resource was first raised in the context of the budgetary burden of the UK after its accession to the Union, and it provided grounds for the compensation and reimbursement measures in favour of the UK (see the section "The UK rebate, at the crossroads of any reform"). In this context the MacDougal report has indicated that being an indirect tax, the VAT resource tends:

first recognised in the 1988 Own Resources Decision.[116] The intention was clearly to allow for an adjustment of the disparities in economic structures (differences in the proportion of member states' GNP accounted for by consumption, and thus in the VAT base). Therefore, instead of increasing the VAT call rate (as previously envisaged to deal with the problem of the exhaustion of own resources), the Decision introduced a GNI-based resource "with a view to matching the resources paid by each member state more closely with its ability to contribute".[117]

The Decision also established the principle that a member state's VAT base could not exceed 55% of its GNP at market prices (the capping mechanism). As a consequence, the VAT-based own resource was turned into a GNI-based resource for the numerous countries that were concerned by the capping rule.[118]

Equity being understood to mean proportionality with GNI, other measures were taken in subsequent Own Resources Decisions in order

---

to have a somewhat regressive incidence, but this distributive problem has broadly speaking been dealt with by the 'Financial Mechanism', which reimburses to economically weaker member states, in certain circumstances and in a certain degree, the excess of their share in total Own Resource payments over their share in Community GNP; this puts the Own Resource system onto an approximately neutral basis from the distributive stand-point. (European Commission, 1977, p. 64)

[116] See Council Decision 88/376/EEC, Euratom of 24 June 1988 on the system of the Communities own resources, OJ L 185, 15.7.1988.

[117] Ibid., see the 10th successive para. introduced by "Whereas".

[118] The percentage of capping does not result from any specific criteria. As shown by its successive gradual reduction, this percentage is purely based on a burden-sharing deal among the member states. In the 2007 EU budget, the capping of the VAT base is applicable to 11 member states (see Table 3.1) and the draft preliminary budget for 2008 foresees its application to two further member states (Latvia and Poland). It is worth noting that the present rules do not exempt member states whose VAT base is capped from making the complicated calculations underlying the VAT resource. Consequently, the Commission carries out the corresponding controls. This task may appear redundant, although it might prove useful in cases where revisions of national accounts show afterwards that the VAT base capping is no longer justified and that adjustments in the VAT resource 'weighted average rate' are needed (see footnote 188 for the Greek case).

gradually to convert the GNI resource into the main source of revenue for financing the Community. In 1992, member states declared "their intention of taking greater account of the contributive capacity of individual member states in the system of own resources, and of examining means of correcting, for the less prosperous member states, regressive elements existing in the present own resources system".[119] Unsurprisingly, the 1994 Own Resources Decision, which transposes into law the Protocol, further reduced the capping of the VAT base to 50% of GNP and provided for a gradual return to the limit of a 1% VAT resource call rate.[120]

This call rate was further reduced by the 2000 Own Resources Decision (to 0.75% as of 2002 and to 0.5% as of 2004), "in order further to continue the process of making allowance for each member state's ability to contribute to the system of own resources and of correcting the regressive aspects of the current system for the least prosperous member states".[121]

With the new financial perspective, the European Council cut the call rate of the VAT resource from 0.5% to 0.3% as of 2007 onwards.[122]

Figure 2.1 presents the evolution of the VAT resource and shows its sharp decline since 1995 in the share of the EU's budget financing.[123]

---

[119] See the Protocol on Economic and Social Cohesion attached to the Maastricht Treaty. It is interesting to note that exactly the same wording was repeated (para. 8) in the Protocol on Economic, Social and Territorial Cohesion attached to the Treaty establishing a Constitution for Europe of 2004.

[120] See Council Decision 94/728/EC, Euratom of 31 October 1994 on the system of the European Communities' own resources, OJ L 293, 12.11.1994. The cap at 50% of the VAT base, which is still applicable, was set from 1995 onwards for Greece, Spain, Ireland and Portugal, and in equal steps over the period 1995 to 1999 for the other member states.

[121] See Council Decision 2000/597/EC, Euratom of 29 September 2000 (op. cit.).

[122] See Council Decision 2007/436/EC/Euratom of 7 June 2007 (op. cit.), which is not yet in force, pending ratification by the member states. The constitutional implications of the Own Resources Decision are explained in footnote 9.

[123] It should be noted that the reduction of the VAT resource share in EU budget financing is partly explained by a lower call rate than the maximum authorised. See also the section "Is the size of the budget a major issue?".

Figure 2.1 Evolution of the VAT resource in financing the EU budget 1992–2006

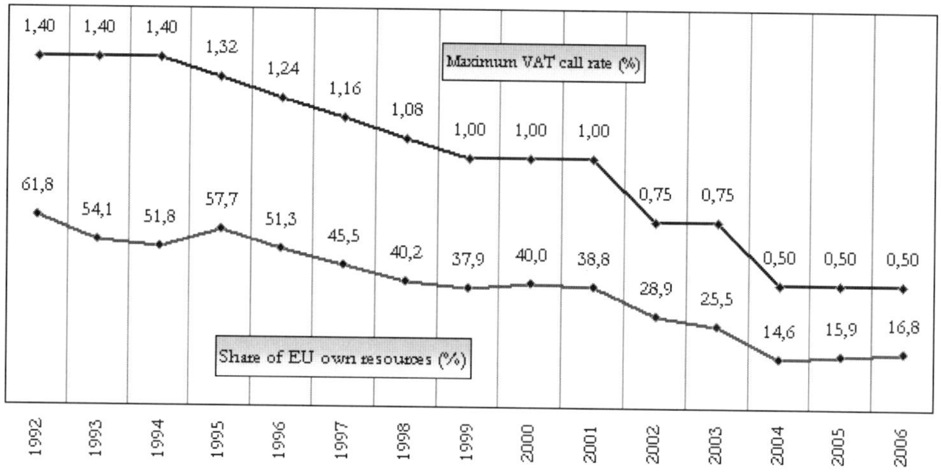

Source: Own Resources Decisions and European Commission (2007l).

If the objective of making the VAT resource the main item of EU budgetary revenue failed owing to the 'sin of regressivity', the aim of establishing a link with the Community taxpayer through this resource fared no better. After an initial possibility to calculate the VAT resource directly from taxable persons' returns, the system was modified so as to make unnecessary any link with taxpayers, and hence with individual consumers and indeed citizens (see Box 2.1). Taxable persons are subject to the tax rules of their member states: they have no 'fiscal' liability vis-à-vis the EU budget.[124]

---

[124] See also footnote 109. An indirect proof of the willingness of the member states to exclude any link whatsoever with taxable persons can be found in the declaration attached to the Brussels Treaty (the Treaty amending Certain Financial Provisions of the Treaty establishing the European Communities and of the Treaty establishing a Single Council and a Single Commission of the European Communities (1975)), which sets up the European Court of Auditors. Concerning customs duties and the other levies, the declaration stated that the Court's audit "shall not cover substantive transactions properly so called shown in the supporting documents which relate to such establishment; accordingly, the audit on the spot shall not be carried out by recourse to the debtor".

Box 2.1 The VAT resource assessment base

The determination of the assessment base for the VAT resource was introduced by Council Regulation (EEC, Euratom, ECSC) No. 2892/77 of 19 December 1977 implementing in respect of own resources accruing from value added tax the Decision of 21 April 1970 on the replacement of financial contributions from member states by the Communities' own resources (OJ L 336, 27.12.1977). Member states could either calculate the VAT assessment base directly from taxable persons' tax returns (the returns method) or indirectly (the revenue method) by dividing net VAT receipts by the weighted average rate of VAT. This intermediate base had to be subsequently adjusted, with negative or positive compensations, in order to obtain a harmonised VAT base corresponding to the provisions in the Sixth Directive of 17 May 1977. The weighted average rate depends on statistical calculations to take account of the different VAT rates applicable to the various categories of taxable goods and services. Hence, the revenue method reconstructs a fictitious tax distinct from that actually paid by consumers in the various member states. The returns method proved to be less favourable to the member states (it was initially chosen only by Denmark and Ireland), as the VAT resource was not linked to VAT actually collected by the member states, but to VAT due (potentially higher than VAT collected). As a result, the revenue method became the practice. Council Regulation (EEC, Euratom) No. 1553/89 of 29 May 1989 on the definitive uniform arrangements for the collection of own resources accruing from value added tax (OJ L 155, 7.6.1989) fixed the revenue method as the definitive one. In this respect, a European Parliament report* raised what it considered a 'fundamental political question': "Can Parliament tolerate the fact that revenue from VAT is being increasingly watered down to a national financial contribution following the necessary abandonment of the principle of the uniform VAT rate and can it accept that the establishment of the uniform VAT base is ultimately reduced to a statistical calculation? Or must every effort be made in connection with the calculation of the VAT base to revive the Communities' own resources system and the financial autonomy of the Community which is dependent thereupon?"

---

* See the Report on behalf of the Committee on Budgets on the Commission's proposal for a Regulation extending the term of validity of Regulation No. 2892/77 and on the report from the Commission on the implementation of Council Regulations Nos. 2891/77 and 2892/77, A2-126/85, Rapporteur: P. Cornelissen, 21 October 1985, point 15, p. 13.

As remarked earlier, the downgrading of the VAT resource has been formally justified by its regressive impact. Nevertheless, it is curious to observe that the last cut in the call rate, which was decided upon in 2005, was made "in the interests of transparency and simplicity" while, at the same time, the Council decided a different call rate for four member states to reduce their budgetary burden.[125]

This further reduction is actually only a confirmation of the tendency since 1988 to increase the GNI-based part of EU's budget financing. One should not exclude the possibility that the specific interests of member states, aiming at diminishing their share in the financing of the budget, played a role in the downgrading of the VAT resource. In this connection, Table 2.2 evaluates the theoretical impact, by member state, of replacing the current VAT resource by the own resource based on GNI.

Member states with a share in total EU GNI that is higher (lower) than their share in the total EU-capped VAT base would lose (gain) from the replacement of the VAT resource by the GNI-based resource.[126] As may be observed, most of the member states would benefit from the replacement of the VAT resource by the GNI resource. It is therefore no surprise that the Council concluded, "a broad majority of delegations are favourable to the idea of switching to a GNI-based system from the current system based on VAT receipts".[127] It should be pointed out that the overall impact of such a shift would be fairly limited at present, owing to the low share of the VAT-based own resource in the total financing of the EU budget.[128] It seems clear, however, that the VAT resource is only being kept alive by the simple fact that a change in the current financing system requires the unanimous agreement of the 27 EU governments.

---

[125] See Council Decision 2007/436/EC/Euratom of 7 June 2007 (op. cit.), the seventh successive para. introduced by "Whereas" and Art. 2(4). See also the section "The price of unanimity: A system of financial deals".

[126] A '+' ('-') in column 6 of Table 2.2 means a gain (loss) if the VAT resource is replaced by the GNI-based resource.

[127] See Ecofin Council Conclusions, 14429/04, Brussels, 16 November 2004(a), p. 9.

[128] This low impact is even accentuated by the 'capping mechanism', following which more than one-third of this resource is actually calculated on the basis of GNI.

Table 2.2 Impact by member state of replacing the VAT resource by the GNI-based resource (2005 EU budget)
(in € million unless otherwise indicated)

Member states	VAT payments	Share in total VAT based payments (= share in EU-capped VAT base) (%)	GNI-based payments	Share in total GNI-based payments (= share in EU GNI) (%)	GNI payments required to replace VAT resource	Difference by member state	In % of total VAT- and GNI-based payments (excl. UK rebate payments)
	(1)	(2)	(3)	(4)	(5)	(6)=(1)-(5)	(7)=(6)/((1)+(3))
Czech Rep.	130.2	0.85	607.2	0.78	119.8	10.3	1.40
Estonia	13.3	0.09	62.1	0.08	12.2	1.1	1.40
Greece	276.5	1.81	1,289.5	1.66	254.5	22.0	1.40
Spain	1,313.8	8.58	6,127.0	7.90	1,209.4	104.4	1.40
Ireland	197.8	1.29	922.4	1.19	182.1	15.7	1.40
Cyprus	20.2	0.13	94.0	0.12	18.6	1.6	1.40
Luxembourg	36.8	0.24	171.6	0.22	33.9	2.9	1.40
Hungary	130.9	0.85	610.4	0.79	120.5	10.4	1.40
Malta	7.3	0.05	33.9	0.04	6.7	0.6	1.40

54 | GABRIELE CIPRIANI

Poland	303.8	1.98	1,416.9	1.83	279.7	24.2	1.40
Portugal	216.4	1.41	1,009.0	1.30	199.2	17.2	1.40
Slovenia	42.7	0.28	198.9	0.26	39.3	3.4	1.40
UK	2,948.1	19.25	13,748.9	17.72	2,713.8	234.4	1.40
Netherlands	709.1	4.63	3,446.1	4.44	680.2	28.9	0.69
France	2,458.8	16.06	12,275.7	15.82	2,423.0	35.8	0.24
Austria	348.0	2.27	1,740.7	2.24	343.6	4.4	0.21
Slovak Rep.	49.4	0.32	254.3	0.33	50.2	-0.8	-0.26
Lithuania	26.1	0.17	136.7	0.18	27.0	-0.9	-0.57
Latvia	14.8	0.10	78.4	0.10	15.5	-0.6	-0.69
Germany	3,044.0	19.88	16,331.2	21.05	3,223.5	-179.5	-0.93
Finland	209.2	1.37	1,123.0	1.45	221.7	-12.5	-0.94
Sweden	388.7	2.54	2,100.7	2.71	414.6	-25.9	-1.04
Italy	1,811.1	11.83	10,171.1	13.11	2,007.6	-196.5	-1.64
Belgium	371.0	2.42	2,156.3	2.78	425.6	-54.6	-2.16
Denmark	245.7	1.60	1,477.0	1.90		-45.9	-2.66
Total	15,313.5	100.00	77,583.0	100.00	15,313.5	0.0	0.00

Source: European Commission (2005d).

Concluding remarks

In 1998 the Court of Auditors noted,

> The VAT resource poses a problem of consistency. If it is to be considered a contribution by the member states, it should logically have been abolished in 1988 and replaced by the GNP resource. If, on the other hand, it is meant to be a tax on the final consumption of European citizens, capping it in accordance with GNP may reasonably be questioned. Indeed, in the latter case, it should be considered a genuine own resource, and capping it would therefore not be justified because that would nullify its primary function. [The Court concluded,] A resource based on the taxable consumption of citizens only has a raison d'être if it is based directly on a tax base declared by the taxpayers.[129]

These conclusions remain relevant today.

Does a VAT-based tax have a future?

Over the years, the European Parliament has been considered the main advocate of an EU tax, in particular a VAT-based resource. In 1981, in a context close to the exhaustion of available resources, the Parliament tried to avert a return to the pre-1970 system of national contributions by requesting that "VAT should no longer be collected on the basis of statistical estimates, but on the basis of tax declarations...so that this source of revenue becomes a veritable Community VAT...levied at separate rates, independent of the national VAT rates". [130] This stance was pursued by Horst Langes who, as rapporteur for the Committee on Budgets, extensively developed the possible introduction of a VAT-based resource.[131] These proposals finally led the Parliament, more than 10 years ago, to come out in favour of a new own resources system "guided by the

---

[129] See European Court of Auditors (1998), paras 3.16 and 5.5.

[130] See European Parliament, Resolution of 9 April 1981 on the Community's own resources, para 13.

[131] See the European Parliament, *Report on a New System of Own Resources for the European Union*, A3-0060/94, Rapporteur: H. Langes, 7 February 1994(a) and the *Report on the System of Own Resources in the European Union*, A3-0228/94, Rapporteur: H. Langes, 8 April 1994(b).

criteria of direct revenue-raising, equal, direct and equitable European taxation, transparency and identifiability".[132] And, despite some hesitations expressed in the past concerning the regressive effect of VAT,[133] it decided to propose more specifically the creation, in place of the existing VAT and GNP resources, of a new source of revenue "which should take the form of a specified percentage of VAT ... directly imposed on the basis of tax declarations and denoted as such on invoices".[134]

The Parliament gave several reasons for such a choice. VAT was considered to represent the most reliable basis for own revenue, to be politically controllable, well known and familiar to the taxpayer and capable of being harmonised throughout the Community. According to the Parliament, a true VAT resource would represent a simple and transparent way of establishing a link between the taxpayer and the destination of the tax. VAT revenue "is politically defensible as its yield is dependent on economic activity and economic growth" and, interestingly, "if national economies stagnate...both the member states and the Union would have to economise".[135] Moreover, this would help to correct misperceptions about the costs of the EU. A fiscal VAT resource would also have the advantage of being flexible, as it could be increased as the range of tasks expands.

The position of the Parliament has evolved since then; its support for a tax-based resource has become less clear-cut, probably as a result of a certain degree of realism.[136] For example, in 1999 the Parliament reaffirmed

---

[132] See European Parliament, Resolution of 9 February 1994 on the system of the Communities' own resources, the amendment introduced as new Recital 17a.

[133] See footnote 115.

[134] See European Parliament, Resolution of 21 April 1994 on a new system of own resources for the European Union, paras 9 and 10.

[135] See European Parliament 1994(a), point 24, p. 15. According to the rapporteur, the consequence of a genuine own resources system would be that eventual surpluses would remain at the EU's disposal (now they correspondingly reduce the own resources call rate for the following year) and unforeseen deficits would be the responsibility of the Union to be met by its own credit financing, although temporarily and under strict conditions. According to the present rules, EU revenue and payment appropriations must be in balance (see footnote 11).

[136] The Parliament observed recently that all its "efforts to use the actual VAT returns to determine the assessment base to be used for the VAT resource ('returns method') instead of the harmonised base calculated by applying an average

that "the budget should be based on new own revenue not constituting member state contributions".[137] Nevertheless, one year later, a large majority did not follow its budgetary committee whose intention was to support initiatives "for a possible introduction of a European tax as a direct revenue which does not lead to additional costs for the taxpayer and could strengthen the link between the Union and its citizens".[138]

However that may be, in its 2004 own resources report, the Commission in practice endorsed the Langes proposal. The Commission expressed its view as below:

> A genuinely fiscal VAT resource would be implemented through an EU rate as part of the national VAT rate paid by taxpayers. It would imply a specific percentage rate of VAT that would be levied for the benefit of the EU. The rate would be incorporated in, and levied together with, the national rate and thus on the same taxable base. Citizens would not have to support an additional tax burden as the Community rate would be offset by an equivalent decrease of the national VAT rate. For example, if the national VAT rate is 21%, and assuming the introduction of an EU rate of 1%, the national rate would come to 20%. The total VAT rate levied would still be 21%. For visibility purposes, the Community VAT and national VAT should appear as separate taxes on the invoice or receipt that a taxable person provides to his customer.[139]

---

weighted rate on the total net revenue ('revenue method') were in vain, with the result that the VAT resource changed from a genuine own resource with a strong direct link to European citizens to a purely statistical device for calculating a contribution of a member state". See European Parliament, Resolution of 29 March 2007 (op. cit.), para. D. Concerning the method of calculation of the VAT resource, see Box 2.1.

[137] See European Parliament, Resolution of 11 March 1999 (op. cit.), para. 9.

[138] See the report by Jutta Haug, European Parliament, *Report on the situation concerning the European Union's own resources in 2001*, A5-0238/2001, 26 June 2001, p. 8, para. 11. At that time, the Belgian government expressed its intention of defining a new budgetary framework over the medium term, during the Belgian presidency, which could lead to discussions on the desirability of a European tax.

[139] See European Commission, *Technical Annex, Financing the European Union, Commission report on the operation of the own resources system*, Vol. II, COM(2004) 505 final, Brussels, 14 July 2004(g), p. 54. The Commission also observed,

Thus, member states would transfer to the EU budget the same percentage of each national VAT base. According to the Commission, the implementation of a VAT-based resource would be feasible over the medium term, with the intention being to replace the current VAT resource by a genuinely tax-based own resource by 2014.

In its 2004 own resources report, the Commission also developed seven criteria for assessing own resources.[140] While the Commission observes that "it is virtually impossible for individual own resources to satisfy all criteria",[141] it seems clear that a real fiscal VAT resource would easily meet criteria such as visibility and simplicity (the Community VAT and national VAT could appear as separate taxes on the invoice or receipt that a taxable person provides to his/her customer), financial autonomy (it would be possible to create independent revenues for the Community as already proposed by the Commission in 1965), sufficiency and stability (VAT is a buoyant and relatively stable source of revenue), efficient allocation of resources and cost-effectiveness (VAT exists already and it is the sole European tax for which the base harmonisation is quite advanced. As a result, no modification of the structure of prices or of the behaviour of economic agents should be expected).

If the above six criteria are doubtless met by a fiscal VAT resource, what about 'equity' and the concerns expressed in the past about the

---

Tax base harmonisation in the field of VAT is quite advanced and it is a sufficient and stable source of revenue. A fiscal VAT resource would make the financing of the EU highly visible to EU citizens. It would also be evolutionary, since it would entail a reform of existing provisions rather than the introduction of a completely new resource. From an administrative point of view, its introduction would not present any insurmountable difficulties. ...Strengthening the direct link of citizens to the budget would also help focussing expenditure debates on substance rather than on purely 'national' budget 'net positions'. (European Commission, Vol. I, 2004f, p. 13)

It is worth mentioning that already in 1998 the Commission considered that among the different options for a tax-based own resource, "[o]nly actual VAT, as proposed by the European Parliament in 1994, would appear to be a solution which could be considered for the medium term". See the speech by Jacques Santer to the European Parliament (Santer, 1998).

[140] See European Commission (Vol. II, 2004g), Annex I.

[141] Ibid., p. 11.

regressive effects of VAT? In this respect, one should first note that, as shown by Figure 2.2, the structure and evolution of member states' taxation systems record a predominance of indirect taxes. Furthermore, this tendency has been accentuated by the upward trend in the taxation of consumption since 2001, both for the EU-25 as a whole and for the subgroup of the EU-15.[142]

Figure 2.2 Evolution of direct/indirect taxation (EU-25 and EU-10 – GDP weighted average), 1995–2004 (%)

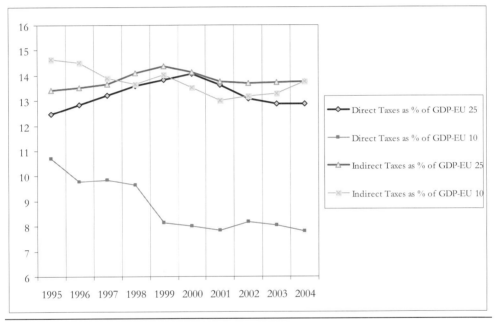

Source: European Commission (2006f).

One might therefore wonder why VAT regressivity, which is not uncontroversial,[143] should be a major issue for the EU budget, when this is apparently not the case for the almost 50 times larger national budgets.

---

[142] For an analysis of the taxation structure, see European Commission, *Structures of the taxation systems in the European Union: 1995–2004*, Doc. Taxud e4/2006/doc/3201, Brussels, 2006(f).

[143] See footnote 115.

In addition, if there is no apparent reason to differentiate between the types of taxation financing the national budgets and the EU budget, there is equally no reason to discriminate between different indirect taxes. If VAT is regressive, it is just as regressive as other indirect taxes such as customs duties, which, moreover, also automatically increase the final price as their value is naturally incorporated into a product's price, which is subject to subsequent VAT taxation. Nobody has thought of accusing customs duties of regressivity, even when they ensured the financing of a larger share of the EU budget.

Equity should be assessed on the assumption that the 'owners' of the EU budget are the European citizens (and taxpayers) and not just their governments. In this context, a fiscal VAT resource will clearly fulfil the criterion of 'horizontal equity' (final consumption could be taxed everywhere in the EU, at the same percentage, for the benefit of the EU budget). Concerning 'vertical equality' or the citizens' ability to pay, one could first observe the relative small size of the EU budget. Second, nothing would prevent lower VAT rates from being set on essential goods.[144] Finally, any budgetary imbalances should in principle find a solution on the expenditure side of the budget. This is in line with the Fontainebleau principle, according to which "expenditure policy is ultimately the essential means of resolving the question of budgetary imbalances".[145]

It therefore seems difficult to find an objective reason to rule out a fiscal VAT resource on the grounds of a supposed lack of equity. If, however, the above considerations tend to support the technical feasibility of a fiscal VAT resource, one should also consider whether such a resource would be at all politically acceptable.

---

[144] This idea was suggested for example by the European Parliament report (1994b), point 26, p. 15. The rapporteur also envisaged, in view of greater tax fairness, the possible introduction of an adjustment mechanism based on GNP (see point 30).

[145] See European Council, Conclusions of the Session of the European Council at Fontainebleau, 25-26 June 1984. The Council Decision 2000/597/EC, Euratom of 29 September 2000 (op. cit.) reaffirmed that budgetary imbalances should be resolved, to the extent possible, by means of expenditure policy (see the 11th successive para. introduced by "Whereas"). See also the section "The UK rebate, at the crossroads of any reform".

The option of superseding the present national contributions by a real fiscal resource to finance the EU budget has been regularly raised in different fora for at least 40 years.[146] Many proposals have been made but none has found the required unanimous support. The issue of an EU tax was last discussed in the context of the European Convention. The idea again proved controversial. On one side were the advocates of the principle of people consenting to taxes, which is at the heart of democracy; on the other side were those who expressed reservations because of the differences in taxation in the member states and the danger of providing Eurosceptic public opinion with more ammunition. Indeed, it has been claimed that "an EU tax would inevitably be seen as an additional burden, would be deeply unpopular in its own right, and would reduce popular support for the EU",[147] and that "it is through maintaining the current dominant role of the member states for budget revenues, rather than providing for a European tax or participation in national taxes, that transparency and legitimacy of budget revenues is best secured".[148]

It would be naïve to expect that the idealistic objective of establishing a link with the European citizen would take precedence over fundamental issues such as member states' fiscal sovereignty or more prosaic ones, such as the impact on burden-sharing. In this respect, the simulations provided by the Commission show that for several member states there is a considerable difference between their share in a fiscal resource based on

---

[146] In 1965, the Commission proposed to allow the European Parliament (once directly elected) to create independent sources of revenue for the Community (see European Commission, 1965). Among others, the issue has been examined for example by the study group on the role of public finance in European integration chaired by D. MacDougal (European Commission, 1977) and by the Reflection Group for preparing the 1996 Intergovernmental Conference chaired by Carlos Westendorp. For a review of possible tax-based EU own resources see Cattoir (2004).

[147] See European Convention, "Discussion circle" on own resources: Response from Lord Tomlinson to the questions put to the Discussion Circle on Own Resources, Working Document 2, CONV 654/03, Brussels, 8 April 2003(b).

[148] See European Convention, "Discussion circle" on own resources: Note from Peter Hain, Member of the Convention – Comments on Secretariat Note describing the system of own resources (Cercle 3, WD 01), Working Document 4, Brussels, 11 April 2003(c).

VAT and both the present VAT resource and a levy based on GNI.[149] It is maybe for this very reason that at the Council, where a broad majority is in favour of a unique GNI-based system, "delegations did not express support for the Commission's idea of introducing a new tax-based EU own resource".[150]

The European Parliament does not indulge in vain hopes either. A recent Resolution recognised "that the time for a new European tax has not yet come in the short term". The Parliament called therefore for a gradual approach, in two stages "but which should form part of a single decision", whereby in the short term the financing of the EU budget would be ensured by traditional own resources and the GNI resource, abolishing the VAT resource in its current form. The Parliament "recognises that the GNI resource is less visible for citizens but equitable in relating contributions to the general level of prosperity of member states and an expression of solidarity between them". It "emphasises, however, the temporary nature of such a phase, in that its sole aim would be to prepare the ground for the introduction of a genuinely new own resources system" in a second phase, "based on a tax already levied in the member states, the idea being that this tax, partly or in full, would be fed directly into the EU budget as a genuine own resource, thus establishing a direct link between the Union and European taxpayers".[151]

This recent position of the European Parliament is actually in line with its previous statements,[152] in particular concerning the fact that a "new system must not increase overall public expenditure nor the tax burden for citizens", that "the ceiling of 1.24% of GNI which already allows for a sizeable margin of manoeuvre" should be maintained and, finally, that "a reform of the structure of EU revenue and a reform of the structure of EU expenditure have to go hand in hand".[153]

---

[149] See European Commission (Vol. II, 2004g), pp. 55–56.

[150] See the Ecofin Council Conclusions (2004a), p. 9.

[151] See European Parliament, Resolution of 29 March 2007 (op. cit.), paras 10, 23, 26, 37 and 38.

[152] See for example European Parliament, Resolution of 11 March 1999 (op. cit.).

[153] See European Parliament, Resolution of 29 March 2007 (op. cit.), paras 30, 32 and 34.

The position of the Parliament has nonetheless evolved on one fundamental issue, namely fiscal sovereignty. In 1994, the Parliament stressed that

> the transfer to the Community of an increasing number of political powers in fields such as agricultural policy, external trade, internal trade, development aid, transport and social policy and economic and monetary policy should go hand in hand with corresponding action to provide the Union with democratic legislative powers, which would include both tax and budgetary powers and appropriate financial autonomy ('no representation without taxation').[154]

It took a similar position a few years later, by claiming full budgetary powers over both expenditure and revenue and emphasising that increasing the EU's financial endowment "also means giving the Union clear responsibility for the relevant fiscal legislation, including appropriate power to raise revenue".[155] Concerning such a claim for EU fiscal independence, a recent Resolution has since dispelled any suspicion. The Parliament has indeed stressed full respect for the principle of the fiscal sovereignty of the member states, "who might, however, authorise the Union, for a limited period to be revoked at any time, to benefit directly from a certain share of a tax as is the case in most member states with regional or local authorities".[156]

This result is the likely one of a pragmatic approach. The Parliament might hope that giving up any claim to EU direct fiscal sovereignty would

---

[154] See European Parliament, Resolution of 21 April 1994 (op. cit.), para. 21.

[155] See European Parliament, Resolution of 11 March 1999 (op. cit.), paras 8 and 9. The principle of giving to the European Parliament full budgetary powers in both expenditure and revenue was reaffirmed in 2000, in the framework of the Intergovernmental Conference, where the Parliament observed that the level of the Union's own resources "should be fixed by Parliament acting in codecision with the Council" (See European Parliament, Resolution of 13 April 2000 containing the European Parliament's proposals for the Intergovernmental Conference, para. 51.4).

[156] See European Parliament, Resolution of 29 March 2007 (op. cit.), para. 29. In this way, the Parliament finally did not endorse the definition of 'own resources' as a "source of finance separate and independent of the member states" and a "tax revenue assigned once and for all to the Community", which was given by the Lamassoure report (see footnote 108). On the issue of fiscal sovereignty, see Castagnède (2002).

facilitate an increase in the Parliament's powers on another sensitive issue: its present very limited role in revenue arrangements, in particular concerning the sources and the volume of the EU's budget revenue.

Concluding remarks

It seems rather clear that, in comparison with other possible forms of taxation, VAT has an advantage over other taxes as a potentially genuine fiscal resource for the EU budget. The key issue in this regard seems to be how (and by whom) the call rate will finally be set and whether the EU institutions will have a direct power of control over the taxable persons. For the member states, the EU's VAT future may represent a greater challenge for their fiscal sovereignty than for the financial impact on their contributions.

3.   EXCEPTION AS THE RULE, TO EACH HIS OWN

If the EU budget suffers from a number of weaknesses, they do not derive from conceptual 'mistakes' made by those (the Commission and the member states) who have set up the current architecture. These peculiarities of the EU budget simply reflect the incompleteness of European integration and the fact that the EU is still pre-eminently an intergovernmental organisation. Although much more advanced than traditional international organisations like the United Nations, it is still far from models like the US. Thus, a reform of the EU budget cannot be conceived in isolation, as a technical question confined to specialists.

These weaknesses, of which some examples are provided below, are the inevitable result of a series of tortuous horse-tradings among member states. The evolution of the EU's budget financing shows that, contrary to the expectations of the EEC Treaty, not only has it not evolved from a system of national contributions towards one of genuine EU own resources, but also owing to the different exceptions and specific arrangements introduced over the years, the system is in reality the outcome of merely intergovernmental deals.

The price of unanimity: A system of financial deals

The history of EU financing is full of examples where specific arrangements have been introduced to accommodate the claims of one member state or another, the UK rebate being just the best known. Each new financial perspective deal provides the opportunity to include specific adjustments to both revenue and expenditure. The consequence is a system that suffers from instability and is not applicable to all member states in the same way.

As the Commission points out, "Past adjustments to accommodate specific interests have added to the system's opaqueness."[157] Along the same lines, the European Parliament has observed that the derogation regimes that have been added to the current own resources system "have only made it more complex, more opaque for citizens and increasingly less equitable and have led to a financing system which has resulted in unacceptable inequalities between member states".[158]

Here are some examples of corrections and derogations on the revenue side:

- The UK rebate, applicable since 1986, consists of reducing by two-thirds the negative balance between the UK's contribution to the budget and the EU's expenditure on the UK.

- In principle, the cost of the UK rebate is to be borne by the other member states through a corresponding increase in their contributions to the EU budget. Yet since the entry into force of the rebate, Germany has been allowed to pay only two-thirds of its normal share, the balance being divided among the other member states on the same scale. As of 1 January 2002, the European Council again altered the scale for financing the UK rebate, by reducing the share paid by Germany, the Netherlands, Austria and Sweden to a quarter of what it ought to be. Consequently, these reductions are again made up by all the other member states.[159]

- Because of the enlargement, the UK rebate was expected to rise considerably.[160] After an (unsuccessful) attempt by the Luxembourg

---

[157] See European Commission (Vol. I, 2004f), p. 8.

[158] See European Parliament, Resolution of 8 June 2005 (op. cit.), para. L.

[159] As a result, in 2007, Germany bears only 6% of the rebate. France, Italy and Spain altogether bear more than 60%.

[160] As the UK rebate is based on the UK's share in total EU expenditure (in the member states), any increase in the expenditure (in other member states) has the effect of increasing simultaneously the volume of the UK rebate. The Commission estimated that if the correction mechanism had remained unchanged, the rebate would have increased during the period 2007–13 from €4.6 to €7.1 billion/year. The UK would have become (together with Finland) the smallest net contributor to the EU budget. At the Berlin European Council (in March 1999), when the envisaged enlargement to 10 new member states was unanimously agreed, the UK

presidency to limit the 'damages'[161] the UK government finally agreed to reduce the impact of the rebate by €10.5 billion for the period 2007–13.[162] Nevertheless, the UK will not participate in the financing of the costs of enlargement related to agriculture and will only fully participate in other enlargement-related expenditure after a phasing-in period between 2009 and 2011.

- With the intention of limiting the contributions of less well-off member states, since 1988 a member state's VAT base has been capped at a percentage of its GDP to counter the regressive effect of the VAT resource.[163]

- In the framework of the new financial perspective agreement, the European Council concluded that four countries should benefit from reduced rates of call of the VAT resource to reduce their respective budgetary burden. Hence, during the 2007–13 period the rate of call of the VAT resource for Austria is fixed at 0.225%, for Germany at 0.15% and for the Netherlands and Sweden at 0.10%.

- Again, to reduce the budgetary burden for these countries, the European Council also concluded that for the period 2007–13 the

---

obtained an agreement that enlargement-related expenditure would be taken into account when calculating the UK rebate, thus shielding it from most of the financial consequences of enlargement.

[161] The Luxembourg presidency proposed to set the UK rebate at its nominal average over the seven-year period immediately prior to the most recent enlargement (1997–2003), i.e. at around €4.6 billion per year. This proposal was justified by the need to take due account of the substantial changes since the 1984 Fontainebleau agreement such as the considerable decrease in agricultural expenditure as a proportion of the budget, the increase in cohesion expenditure as a result of enlargement to states with substantially lower levels of prosperity and the rise in the UK's relative prosperity to amongst the highest in the Union (see European Council, Presidency Note, "Financial Perspective 2007–2013", 10090/05, Brussels, 15 June 2005(b)).

[162] The UK rebate is thus expected to reach approximately €6 billion averaged over 2007–13. This amount will be adjusted further upwards in case of further enlargement before 2013, except for the accession of Romania and Bulgaria.

[163] On the regressive effect of VAT, see footnote 115. The percentage of capping, initially set at 55%, has been gradually reduced since 1995, down to 50%.

Netherlands shall benefit from a gross annual reduction in its GNI contribution of €605 million and Sweden from a gross annual reduction in its GNI contribution of €150 million.[164]

- As of 2001, the percentage of collection costs refunded to member states in return for collecting the traditional own resources was increased from 10% to 25%. Although of general application, this measure was intended to 'lighten' the contributions to the EU budget of some member states.[165]

Table 3.1 shows that for the financing of the EU budget, exceptions on the revenue side are applied in one way or another to no fewer than 16 member states.

---

[164] These gross reductions will be financed by all member states, i.e. including the Netherlands and Sweden. It was only at the end of long negotiations that a political agreement could be reached in April 2007 as to whether these gross reductions should (in the view of the UK government) or should not (in the view of the other member states) enter into the calculation of the UK rebate. The UK has finally agreed that these gross reductions shall have no impact on the calculation of the rebate.

[165] See European Parliament Resolution of 29 March 2007 (op. cit.), para. M; see also European Commission (Vol. II, 2004g), p. 14. It is indeed hard to believe that such a high rate of refund justifies compensation for the cost of the administrative service. The refund rate has been set irrespective of the actual collection costs (how to calculate the exact costs for each member state would probably become a contentious issue) and the Commission's proposal to link this increase to specific objectives (like the fight against fraud) was rejected by the member states. The main beneficiaries of this increase are Germany, the UK and the Netherlands. Between 1992 and 2005, they have together collected on average 58% of all customs duties. In 2005, they received some €2.2 billion as collection costs, plus interest, penalties and late interest charged to the debtors. It is worth noting that, as a way of increasing the EU's own resources, the Commission proposed (although unsuccessfully) discontinuing this refund 20 years ago (see European Commission, *Report by the Commission to the Council and Parliament on the Financing of the Community Budget*, COM(87) 101, Brussels, 28 February 1987, p. 26).

Table 3.1 Specific arrangements applicable to some member states on revenue (2007-13)

Member states	Capping of the VAT base to 50% of GNI	Reduced call rate of the VAT resource	Abatements	Reduced participation in bearing the cost of the UK rebate
Bulgaria	x			
Czech Republic	x			
Germany		x		x
Estonia	x			
Greece	x			
Spain	x			
Ireland	x			
Cyprus	x			
Luxembourg	x			
Malta	x			
Netherlands		x	x	x
Austria		x		x
Portugal	x			
Slovenia	x			
Sweden		x	x	x
UK			x	

Source: Council Decision 2007/436/EC/Euratom of 7 June 2007.

On the expenditure side, at the European Council of December 2005 supplementary amounts worth €11.2 billion were granted, for different reasons, to a number of regions. In this respect, the European Parliament has stressed that of the 46 articles determining expenditure under the heading of cohesion for growth and employment, "a full 20 are 'additional provisions' handing out 'Christmas presents' freely to various member states or regions".[166] Table 3.2 summarises these special arrangements.

---

[166] See European Parliament, Resolution of 29 March 2007 (op. cit.), para. 13.

Table 3.2 *Specific measures agreed by the European Council in December 2005 on expenditure*

Earmarked for projects	€865 million for the nuclear power plant Ignalina (LT) and €375 million for the nuclear power plant Bohunice (SK)
	€200 million for the peace process in Northern Ireland (UK)
Earmarked for regions	€879 million for five Polish Objective 2 regions (€107 per citizen)
	€140 million for a Hungarian region (Közép-Magyarország)
	€200 million for Prague
	€100 million for the Canary Islands
	€150 million for the Austrian border regions
	€75 million for Bavaria
	€50 million for Ceuta and Melilla (ES)
	€225 million for the eastern German Länder
	€136 million for the most remote regions (€35 per citizen)
	€150 million for the Swedish regions under the Competitiveness and Employment Objective
Special funds for member states	€2,000 million for Spain, to be distributed freely among the Structural Fund Objectives
	€1,400 million for Italy (predefined distribution)
	€100 million for France (Regional Competitiveness and Employment Objective)
	€47 million for Estonia (€35 per citizen)
	€81 million for Lithuania (€35 per citizen)
Additional payments from rural development	€1,350 million for Austria
	€820 million for Sweden
	€500 million for Ireland
	€460 million for Finland
	€500 million for Italy
	€320 million for Portugal
	€100 million for France
	€20 million for Luxembourg

Source: European Parliament, Resolution of 29 March 2007 (op. cit.), extract from the Annex on the future of the European Union's own resources.

Concluding remarks

The European Parliament has recently remarked that the "numerous exceptions on the revenue side and its compensation gifts to certain member states on the expenditure side, is the clearest proof of the complete failure of the current system".[167] Indeed, in the place of an own resources system the EU budget is financed through a complex arrangement of financial deals on a country-by-country basis. These deals, negotiated in a context where unanimity is required, are pre-eminently based on what the individual governments consider their national interest. In this respect, the priority is often to achieve 'acceptable' net balances rather than specific policy objectives. The focus on budgetary balances tends to overwhelm other policy-oriented considerations.[168]

In need of more than one GNI?

The GNI underlies important decisions on the EU's finances and the utilisation of statistics as 'accounting data' made by the EU budget is unique in the statistical context. This is true on the revenue side, where total own resources are fixed as a percentage of GNI, since the GNI resource constitutes the main source of financing of the EU budget and, finally, the same statistical categories on the basis of the GNI are used in the calculation of the VAT resource.[169] It is also true on the expenditure side, where the GNI (or GDP, from which it is derived) determines the member states' eligibility for the cohesion fund and the regions' eligibility for funding from the structural funds (under the convergence objective), as well as the corresponding financing packages. Moreover, the government deficits and debts of member states are monitored in the framework of the excessive deficit procedure through reference values based on the GDP.[170]

---

[167] Ibid., para. 6.

[168] For the concept of budgetary balances, see the section "Estimating the benefits, a facile solution".

[169] The VAT resource is basically calculated by dividing the total net VAT revenue collected by the weighted average rate of the VAT. The establishment of the VAT weighted-average rate requires a breakdown of transactions by statistical category from national accounts, such as final consumption of private households, intermediate consumption and gross fixed capital formation. See also Box 2.1.

[170] See Art. 104 TEC.

Since it plays such a key role in the EU budget, the legitimacy of the GNI/GDP needs to be beyond dispute, and particularly its use according to the most refined standards and the consequent reliability, exhaustiveness and comparability of the data that are produced by the national statistical offices according to EU rules. As has been observed by the Court of Auditors, "[o]ne might expect that macro-economic aggregates would always be used in their most complete form".[171] Moreover, "when statistics – gross domestic product or inflation, for example – have a financial impact, accuracy and comparability are vital".[172] (See also Box 3.1.)

Box 3.1 European statistics

The EC Treaty states that "the production of Community statistics shall conform to impartiality, reliability, objectivity, scientific independence".* Council Regulation (EC) No. 322/97 of 17 February 1997 on Community Statistics (OJ L 52, 22.2.1997) has established a legislative framework for the systematic and programmed production of Community statistics, the so-called 'Statistical Law'. This Regulation also defines (Art. 10) the principles governing Community statistics. In addition, there is a self-regulatory Code of Practice. The Code was prepared and endorsed by the national statistical institutes. It was promulgated in the Commission recommendation of 25 May 2005 on the independence, integrity and accountability of the national and Community statistical authorities. The Code consists of 15 principles to be applied in connection with the production of Community statistics. It has a dual purpose: on the one hand, to improve trust and confidence in the statistical authorities by proposing certain institutional and organisational arrangements and, on the other hand, to reinforce the quality of the statistics they produce and disseminate, by promoting the coherent application of the best international statistical principles, methods and practices by all producers of official statistics in Europe. The Code of Practice establishes the principle of professional independence in the following terms: "[T]he professional independence of statistical authorities from other policy, regulatory or administrative departments and bodies, as well as from private sector operators, ensures the credibility of European Statistics".** Eurostat is the Community authority responsible for carrying out the tasks devolving on the Commission for producing Community statistics.

---

[171] See European Court of Auditors (1998), para. 3.17.

[172] See Eurostat, *Quality Work and Quality Assurance within Statistics*, 1999 edition, European Commission, Brussels, p. 3.

* See Art. 285(2) of the EC Treaty introduced by the Amsterdam Treaty, the Treaty amending the Treaty on European Union, the Treaties establishing the European Communities and Certain Related Acts) (1997).

** See European Commission, Communication on the Independence, Accountability and Integrity of the National and Community Statistical Authorities, COM(2005) 217 final, Brussels, 25 May 2005(e).

In 1996, a new (1995) version of the European System of Integrated Economic Accounts (ESA 95) was adopted.[173] The new system was meant to "bring an improvement in Community statistics and make them more consistent…[and enable] the financing of the Community budget to be met more adequately".[174] Yet, the legislation expressly prevented this new ESA from being used for the purposes of own resources until a new decision on own resources had been adopted. This was because the Council was aware of the probability "that the new system will involve an increase in Community GNP and a change in the relationships between member states' GNPs".[175]

Indeed, the GNI (ESA 95) was actually some 2% higher in volume when compared with the GNP (the former ESA). The effect on the global amount of resources for the EU budget was 'neutralised' through specific arrangements, but the 'freeze' of ESA 95 in the framework of own resources did result in some significant distributional consequences in the burden-sharing among member states.[176]

---

[173] The 1995 version of the ESA was introduced by Council Regulation (EC) No. 2223/96 of 25 June 1996 (op. cit.), p. 1.

[174] See European Council, Presidency Note, "Progress Report on Statistics", 7057/95, 15 May 1995, p. 2.

[175] Ibid.

[176] The potential increase in the GNP if estimated according to ESA 95 was confirmed by a calculation made by the Commission in 2001 (see European Commission, 2001). This would have represented a theoretical supplementary amount of some €6 billion of own resources. The Own Resources Decision (Council Decision 2000/597/EC, Euratom of 29 September 2000, op. cit., Art. 3) maintained unchanged the amount of financial resources put at the disposal of the Communities by reducing the own resources ceiling from 1.27% (GNP) to 1.24% (GNI), on the basis of a formula of conversion between the old and the new ESA. For the period 1998–2000, the plus/minus differences between member states

The ESA 95 was first applied to the EU own resources in 2002, although with the explicit reservation that if future modifications to the ESA 95 resulted in significant changes in the GNI, the decision concerning whether these modifications should apply to the EU own resources would be taken by the Council, acting unanimously.[177] As a result, a principle of duality between a 'true' GNI and a 'surrogate' for own resources purposes was established. Although there is no reason statistical changes to improve the ESA methodology should not apply in the own resources area.

For example, the GNI version used for the purposes of own resources excludes the subdivision of financial intermediation services indirectly measured (FISIM),[178] for both the establishment of the overall ceiling and

---

amounted globally to €1 billion, with France being the biggest winner (€560 million less than theoretically due if ESA 95 had been applied) and the UK being the main loser (€701 million in excess).

[177] See Council Decision 2000/597/EC, Euratom of 29 September 2000 (op. cit.), Art. 2(7). A similar provision has been inserted into the new Own Resources Decision (see Art. 2(7) of Council Decision 2007/436/EC/Euratom of 7 June 2007, op. cit.). The Council has again reserved itself the right to decide whether (and not when, as proposed by the Commission) the modifications to the ESA methodology should apply to the own resources.

[178] Financial intermediaries provide services for which they charge implicitly by paying or charging different rates of interest to borrowers and lenders. In this situation, the national accounts must use an indirect measure, the FISIM, of the value of the services for which the intermediaries do not charge. In principle, FISIM output should be allocated among the various users of the services for which no explicit charges are made, and therefore in national accounts treated as intermediate consumption by enterprises, as final consumption by households, general government and non-profit institutions serving households or as exports to non-residents. This would ensure that the levels of GDP and GNI take account of FISIM as for any other type of output. But in practice, it may be difficult to find a method of allocating FISIM among different users in a way that is conceptually satisfactory from an economic viewpoint and for which the requisite data are also available. National statistical offices have been required to allocate FISIM in national accounts since 2005. For a review of the topic, see European Commission, *Report Concerning the Allocation of Financial Intermediation Services Indirectly Measured (FISIM) containing a qualitative and quantitative analysis of the results of the trial calculations for allocating and calculating FISIM as described in the Council*

the GNI resource to be paid by each member state. This is so even though "it is broadly recognised that, from a theoretical point of view, allocating FISIM would improve ESA methodology as more accurate GDP levels could be obtained: GDP would include the entire value added generated by financial intermediaries, and not just the part (varying significantly between member states) corresponding to commissions and fees directly invoiced to customers".[179]

In particular, to the extent that FISIM are recorded as final consumption (rather than intermediate consumption) and net exports, GDP levels increase. It has been estimated that the impact of allocating FISIM to GDP (and GNI) would correspond to an increase of 1.3% (weighted average of the countries). Still, it should be stressed that this increase is different from member state to member state.[180] Here again the issue is that a more accurate comparison of GDP levels within the EU would inevitably represent a potential change in the allocation key of the GNI resource.

The European Parliament has recently expressed concern at such a 'dual' GNI.[181] As the European Court of Auditors observed, a discretionary use of the statistical data "offends against the principle of the impartiality

---

Regulation (EC) No. 448/98 of 16 February 1998, COM(2002) 333/F, Brussels, 21 June 2002(b).

[179] See European Commission (2002b), p. 4.

[180] Ibid., pp. 4 and 9–18. It should be observed, incidentally, that this potential increase is close to the overall value of the EU budget.

[181] On the allocation of FISIM, the Parliament has regretted "that the Commission has so far not submitted a proposal to the Council to apply those modifications when calculating the own resources" and that "the Commission evidently takes a different approach from that taken to including illegal activities in GNI…which are included in the calculation of own resources although uniform application by the member states is not ensured and the Commission has therefore notified reservations making it possible to adjust the figures retrospectively" (see European Parliament, Resolution of 24 April 2007, op. cit., paras 91–92). In its response to the Court of Auditors' annual report concerning the financial year 2005 (para. 4.30 (e)), the Commission indicated that it would present a proposal to include allocated FISIM for GNI own resources when it considered that all member states were able to implement this adjustment in a uniform manner, which is expected to occur in 2008.

of Community statistics, which implies that they should be produced in an objective and independent way". The Court thus concluded: "The GNP resource is therefore in danger of becoming a purely financial contribution, ending up as a formula for budgetary cost-sharing among the member states."[182]

Concerning the reliability, exhaustiveness and comparability of the national accounts statistical data, a meaningful and legitimate use at the European level requires the data, which are established by the national statistical offices, to be made comparable using harmonised methodologies. In this respect, Eurostat has the key role in consolidating these data and ensuring that they meet the necessary statistical quality standards. In other words, data should be of high quality and comparable across countries, making it possible to compare apples with apples.[183]

The European Court of Auditors has stressed that:

> the need to guarantee equivalent sources, methods and calculation procedures in the member states means that the GNP must be evaluated in the light of instruments for measuring the quality of the national accounts. Such instruments ought to ensure that the GNP enjoys the legitimacy that the various uses to which it is put within the European Union require.[184]

---

[182] See European Court of Auditors (1998), para. 3.20.

[183] The question of the reliability and comparability of statistical data has been examined in a previous study, which explored the possibility of an indirect assessment through comparison between national accounts data and structural business statistics (for which a reliability rate – 95% – is required). Despite appropriate adjustments, the results showed several unexplained inconsistencies in the 'value added' estimations according to the two sets of data. It was also observed that in the structural business statistics the amount of the intermediate costs was higher compared with that recorded in the national accounts. As structural business statistics could be assumed to be a proxy of taxable persons' returns, this constitutes an index of the undervaluation of the taxable amount by the taxable persons. It seems clear that the cross-checking of statistical data from different sources could only increase their consistency and legitimacy. See Cipriani & Polito (2003).

[184] See European Court of Auditors (1998), para. 5.5.

Several years ago, the Court examined the Commission's control of the reliability and comparability of the member states' GNP data.[185] The concept is summarised by the diagram shown in Figure 3.1.

Figure 3.1 The reliability and comparability of the data

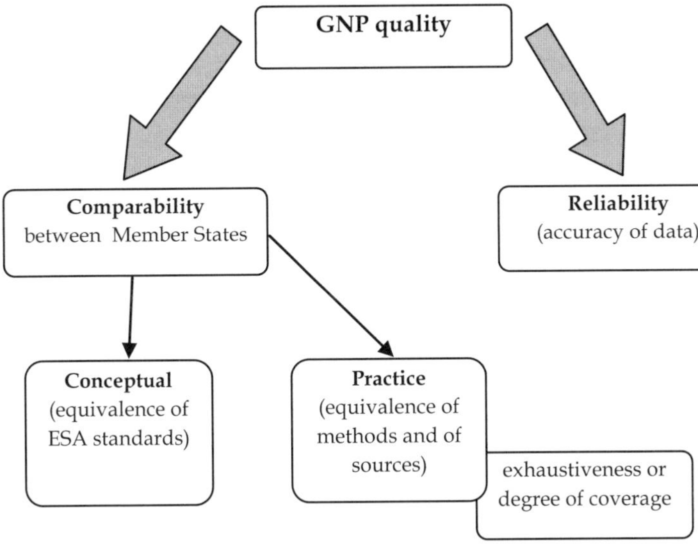

Source: European Court of Auditors (2000), para. 18.

The Court observed that, despite certain improvements, "the Commission has not yet adopted sufficiently transparent analytical procedures for validating the data used in calculating GNP". Verifications are indeed limited to desk checks and relate more specifically to the sources and methods used by member states for the compilation of national accounts' aggregates. The Commission considered, however, "that the regular checks conducted by its departments" and the activities of the GNP Committee "have made it possible to improve the quality and achieve a sufficient degree of comparability of the GNP data of the member states".[186] In 2005, the Court continued to observe insufficient verification by the

---

[185] See European Court of Auditors, *Special Report No. 17/2000 on the Commission's control of the reliability and comparability of the member states' GNP data*, OJ C 336, 27.11.2000.

[186] Ibid., para. 90.

Commission of the underlying national accounts that form the basis for the GNI resource questionnaires.[187]

The difficulties of Eurostat's control of the quality of statistical data have been shown by the monitoring of ESA 95 government accounts in the framework of the excessive deficit procedure. The case of the significant revisions of the Greek deficit and debt figures for the years 2000 to 2003, "of a size and scope that is causing real worries to the Commission",[188] raised not only concerns about the reliability of the deficit and debt figures previously notified but also highlighted the possibility of weaknesses in the monitoring of fiscal statistics.[189]

In reality, the Commission had previously expressed concern at the fact that in several countries "the government accounts are not yet as reliable as they should be and are subject to large revisions" and are "not transparent enough". It also observed that "statistical institutes have scarce resources to compile the government accounts and are not immune from political pressures".[190] The Council supported "a rigorous compliance monitoring of statistics for the Excessive Deficit Procedure and the Stability and Growth Pact, notably based on a full transparency of the concepts, data and methods underlying the compilation of these data" and recognised the need "to strengthen and safeguard trustworthy official statistics". In this perspective, the Council mandated Eurostat to assess "the compliance of

---

[187] See European Court of Auditors, *Annual Report concerning the financial year 2005*, OJ C 263, 30.10.2006(b), para. 4.16.

[188] See European Commission, "Statement by Commissioner Joaquín Almunia on the revision of Greek deficit and debt data", Press release, IP/04/1135, Brussels, 23 September 2004(h). Towards the end of 2004, the Greek budgetary statistics underwent a very large revision. The government deficit for 2003, which was initially reported at 1.7% of GDP, stood at 4.6% of GDP after the September 2004 notification. The deficits notified to the Commission for 2000, 2001 and 2002 were also revised upwards by more than two percentage points of GDP. The government deficit was revised upwards by 2.1% of GDP on average over the period 1997–2003, hence consistently exceeding the 3% ceiling of GDP (see European Commission, *Report on the Accountability Issue related to the Revision of Greek Budgetary Data*, COM(2004) 784, Brussels, 1 December 2004(i), p. 3).

[189] See European Commission, Communication, Towards a European Governance Strategy for Fiscal Statistics, COM(2004) 832, Brussels, 22 December 2004(j), p. 3.

[190] See European Commission (2002c), p. 4.

the reported data with the accounting rules, including the completeness, plausibility and consistency of the data" and asked member states to provide "access to the information required for the purpose of this assessment", including an in-depth examination of the ESA 95 government accounts of each member state.[191] As the Council also noted, "[r]eliable fiscal statistics are essential for the credibility of the excessive deficit procedure" and "on several occasions the fiscal statistics had been revised after a new government took office. The Council considers that the compilation and reporting of statistics for the EDP must not be vulnerable to political and electoral cycles."[192]

Despite its role as a statistical authority,[193] Eurostat has taken the view that it does not have the power to carry out direct controls on member states' government accounts, it cannot oblige the national authorities to provide information that is considered relevant for counterchecking the reported deficit and debt figures, and finally it does not have the power to make on-the-spot verifications of items that may be deemed in need of further clarification.[194]

Actually, the issue seems less 'legal' than one might believe, with the EC Treaty (in particular Arts 104 and 285) providing the logical framework for a more direct involvement of Eurostat in the scrutiny of the data provided. It must be recognised that, especially since 2000, Eurostat has been very active in promoting the quality of statistical data. Still, this is probably not yet sufficient to ensure a proper (and formal) 'validation' of these data by the European statistical authority, without which the use of the GDP/GNI in the framework of the EU budget or in other EU contexts will not have the required credibility and legitimacy. It is encouraging that the Commission is currently discussing with the member states ways in

---

[191] See Ecofin Council Conclusions, 5936/03, Brussels, 18 February 2003, pp. 11 and 34.

[192] See Ecofin Council Conclusions, 9779/04, Brussels, 2 June 2004(b), pp. 10-11.

[193] Council Regulation (EC) No. 322/97 of 17 February 1997 (op. cit.), the Statistical Law, identifies Eurostat as the Community authority. Furthermore, Art. 4 of the Protocol on the Excessive Deficit Procedure, annexed to the Treaty, establishes that the statistical data for the implementation of the excessive deficit procedure "shall be provided by the Commission".

[194] See European Commission (2004i), p. 6.

which verification that is more direct might be carried out, as well as the scope for these checks.[195]

Concluding remarks

The impact of statistics on national accounts has fundamentally changed since their use as accounting data in the framework of the EU budget. In turn, this raises basic issues such as the quality of the data and their comparability across member states and, consequently, the identification of methodological instruments to assess their reliability through transparent validation procedures. There is no alternative but to invite Eurostat to play such a role, which, in the end, is intended to ensure a key precondition of Community statistics: the conceptual and practical comparability of data. In addition, the utilisation of one single GDP/GNI for all different requirements in the EU framework will increase its credibility and legitimacy.

The UK rebate, at the crossroads of any reform

The problem of the UK's budgetary burden is as old as the accession of this member state to the European Community in 1973. This imbalance has been attributed to two factors:

- an agricultural sector that is relatively smaller than and structurally different from those of other member states, thus resulting in lower CAP spending in the UK; and

- a proportionately larger contribution to the financing of the Community budget because the UK's share of the harmonised VAT base was relatively higher than its share of the total GNP of the Community.[196]

The principle of a corrective mechanism to give a payment to a member state that was making a disproportionate contribution to

---

[195] See European Court of Auditors, *Annual Report concerning the financial year 2004*, OJ C 301, 30.11.2005, response to para. 4.30(a). In its report to the Council on the follow-up to the 2005 Discharge Decisions (COM(2007) 537 final, Brussels, 19 September 2007(q), p. 6) the Commission committed itself to "perform more direct verification of selected national aggregates in the sense indicated by the Court during the 2007–2009 round of GNI verification missions".

[196] See European Commission (1998), Annex 4.

Community financing was agreed in 1974,[197] one year after UK's accession and it was formalised at the Dublin summit of March 1975. Although of general application, the mechanism was intended to answer the UK problem. A financial mechanism was introduced in 1976, for a period of seven years based on Art. 235 of the EC Treaty (actions not foreseen by the Treaty).[198] The legal basis was a matter for concern at the time, as this Treaty provision requires the measures to contribute "to the realisation of the objectives of the Community". The obvious risk was that the financial mechanism would be against the *acquis communautaire* represented by the own resources system set up by the Decision of 20 April 1970, as it was a

---

[197] See European Council, Meetings of the Heads of State or Government (Summit) in Paris, 9-10 December 1974.

[198] See Council Regulation (EEC) No. 1172/76 of 17 May 1976 setting up a financial mechanism (OJ L 131, 20.5.1976). A partial reimbursement of a member state's VAT-based contribution would be applied, depending on three conditions to be met simultaneously: GNP per capita of less than 85% of the Community average, growth rate of per capita GNP of less than 120% of the Community average and a member state's share of financing the EU budget that is higher than 10% of its share of the Community GNP. No member state fulfilled the conditions for a payment. This was also because the transitional measures laid down by the Treaty of Accession limited the UK payments to the budget and because the Own Resources Decision of 1970 only came into full effect in 1980. The conditions for the application of the mechanism were relaxed in 1980 solely for the UK (Council Regulation (EEC) No. 2743/80 of 27 October 1980 amending Regulation (EEC) No. 1172/76 setting up a financial mechanism, OJ L 284, 29.10.1980) but they still did not give rise to a payment, particularly owing to the increase in the value of the pound (for a report on the application of the financial mechanism, see European Commission, *Report on the Application of the Financial Mechanism*, COM(81) 704 final, Brussels, 13 November 1981). At the same time, the Council decided that there would be net payments in the form of specific measures on the expenditure side (see Council Regulation (EEC) No. 2744/80 of 27 October 1980 establishing supplementary measures in favour of the United Kingdom, OJ L 284, 29.10.1980 and Council Regulation (EEC) No. 624/83 of 15 March 1983 amending Council Regulation (EEC) No. 2744/80 establishing supplementary measures in favour of the United Kingdom, OJ L 073, 19.3.1983). On this basis, the UK received a net compensation worth €5.6 billion. A flat reduction of €1 billion in the UK's VAT contribution was granted for 1985.

potential threat to the objective of replacing the financial contributions from member states by the Communities' own resources.[199]

Despite several corrections, the mechanism proved to be unsatisfactory as a means of reducing the financial burden to a level that was acceptable for the UK. This gave rise to further negotiations and, finally, to the present UK rebate. This abatement, secured by the UK government in 1984,[200] consists of reducing by two-thirds the negative balance between the UK's contribution to the budget and EU's expenditure on the UK.[201] No link was established to any particular level of agricultural

---

[199] Further developments of this issue have shown that this risk has indeed materialised and that the notion of *juste retour* is now an accepted principle and current practice in negotiations. The issue of the benefits for the member states accruing from the EU budget is examined in the chapter "Budgetary balances – An irresistible temptation".

[200] See European Council (1984). For an analysis of the Fontainebleau agreement, see Denton (1984). The present UK rebate mechanism presents two main differences when compared with the previous period. It is enshrined in the Own Resources Decision and therefore in practice takes on the nature of a permanent mechanism, the modification of which in the future would necessitate the agreement of the UK government. Second, the mechanism is no longer a lump sum, as it was between 1981 and 1985, to be negotiated at regular intervals with the other member states. Being a proportionate and automatic mechanism, it represents for the UK a guarantee that the effects of any future increase of the European budget, especially following an enlargement, will be limited (for the effects of the last enlargement on the level of the UK rebate see footnote 160).

[201] On the revenue side, the calculation of the UK rebate excludes the traditional own resources (customs duties, agricultural levies) from the categories of revenue to be taken into account. This is justified for two reasons. First, traditional own resources are not considered a member state contribution but constitute revenue belonging to the EU by virtue of the customs union. Second, traditional own resources are often levied at the port of entry into the EU in application of the Common Customs Code. Since the final consumer of the imported goods does not necessarily live in the country of the port of entry there is no clear geographical link between the collection of the duties and the economic burden they represent (see European Commission, Vol. II, 2004g, p. 30). On the expenditure side, only the EU's 'allocated expenditure' is taken into account. This is nothing else than the result of the allocation to member states of all EU expenditure that can be attributed to one of them (in practice: agriculture, structural policies, internal policies including research and administrative expenditure). Thus, the definition of

spending in the UK or to any particular level of VAT base at any time.[202] Despite the theoretical application *erga omnes* of such a rebate, the concept of 'excessive' burden remains undefined and "there is no monitoring procedure to examine that the said correction is still justified".[203]

More than 20 years later, the rebate is still applicable and it is legitimate to wonder whether the justifications for granting a correction to the UK are still relevant. It is worth remembering that the European Parliament had rejected the idea of "a Community à la carte in respect of the system of own revenue in which individual states might claim privileges for an indefinite period".[204] On the one hand, according to the Commission, in the absence of any correction mechanism, the UK would have been on average the largest net contributor over the last seven years, and this is probably why the European Council decided to maintain the rebate on all occasions after its reviews in 1988, 1992, 1999 and 2005. On the other hand, as the Commission also points out, economic developments, enlargement and changes in the structure of the EU budget have significantly modified the context in which the existing UK rebate mechanism operates. Incidentally, some indicators suggest that the UK's

---

allocated expenditure excludes any expenditure benefiting recipients outside the EU, in particular external expenditure. Similarly, total allocated expenditure is reduced by an amount equal to pre-accession expenditure in the acceding countries in the last year before enlargement. Allocated expenditure represented in 2005 around 92% of the total €105 billion of EU expenditure. It should be observed that the collection costs for customs, agricultural and sugar levies retained by the member states (around 20% goes to the UK, see also footnote 165) are excluded from the allocated expenditure. This approach is, however, conceptually doubtful, as the European Court of Auditors has pointed out (see Opinion No. 8/99 of 7 October 1999 on a Council proposal for a Decision on concerning the European Union's system of own resources, OJ C 310, 20.10.99, paras 11–19).

[202] In the same way, the establishment of the ceiling for the UK rebate at two-thirds of the negative budgetary balance is purely conventional, and in a way arbitrary. A European Parliament report has described the calculation of the UK rebate as "using a system which is complex and incomprehensible for the politicians in the budgetary authority. It is therefore impossible to judge whether it is sound" (see European Parliament, 1994b, p. 8).

[203] See European Court of Auditors (1998), para. 3.26.

[204] See European Parliament, Resolution of 21 April 1994 (op. cit.), para. 20.

relative degree of prosperity is now much better than it is for other countries that are also net contributors.[205]

The changes in the degree of prosperity enjoyed by EU net contributors are outlined in Table 3.3, which shows the development of GNI per capita, expressed in purchasing power standards (PPS).[206] These data show that the UK's relative prosperity is at the top of the range, in sharp contrast with the situation in 1984, when the UK was the least prosperous of the net contributors.

Furthermore, one should also acknowledge that at least one of the arguments that justified the UK correction is no longer relevant. The VAT resource has been reduced to a very limited share in the financing of the budget. In addition, more than one-third of this resource is actually calculated on the basis of GNI, because of the capping mechanism.[207] As a result, own resources are a function of GNI to the extent of about 76%.

Table 3.3 GNI per capita of net contributors (in PPS) (EU-15 average = 100)

	2003	Comparative rank		1984
UK	111.2	1	5	90.6
Denmark	111.1	2	2	104.0
Austria	109.8	–	–	–
Netherlands	106.6	3	3	95.0
Sweden	104.6	–	–	–
France	104.2	4	2	104.0
Germany	98.6	5	1	109.6
Italy	97.3	6	4	92.9

Source: European Commission (Vol. I, 2004f), p. 5.

[205] In 1998, the Commission stated that it could be envisaged progressively to phase out or to reduce the UK rebate. "This could find a justification in the fact that after enlargement, the relative prosperity of the UK, which is already around the EU average today, would almost certainly be above the EU average, thus weakening one of the conditions for the initial granting of the rebate" (see the European Commission report, 1998, p. 30).

[206] The definition of PPS is given in footnote 83.

[207] In 1986, when the present UK rebate mechanism first entered into force the VAT resources covered 70% of the EU's budget revenue. In 2006, it represented only 17% (see Table 2.1 and Figure 2.1). Moreover, 37% of revenue accruing from VAT resources during that year was calculated on GNI-capped bases.

Concerning agricultural spending, as Figure 3.2 shows, it still takes up a large part of total EU expenditure.[208]

In percentage terms, EU agricultural expenditure on the UK is the lowest among the major member states (see Figure 3.3). Nevertheless, the trend since 1992 has rather been increasing, and for several years it was even at a high level – which shows that the European agricultural policy is not per se 'incompatible' with the UK's agricultural structure.

Figure 3.2 Evolution of EU agricultural expenditure 1992–2006 (%)

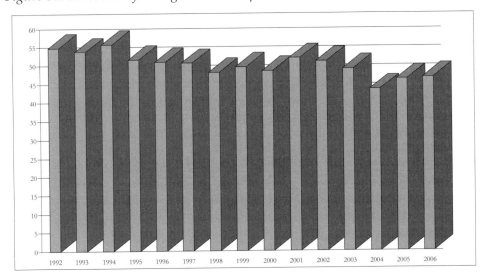

Source: Own calculations based on European Commission (2007l).

---

[208] Agricultural spending represented 71% of the 1975 EU budget. Ten years later, this percentage was down to 68% and it did not represent more than 47% in 2006. For the Financial Perspective 2007–13, agricultural spending (excluding rural development) is expected to account for around one-third of the commitment appropriations foreseen. A fundamental reform of the CAP entered into force in 2004 and 2005. The vast majority of subsidies are now paid independently of the volume of production (83% of the agricultural expenditure proposed in the preliminary draft budget for 2008). More specifically, more money is available to farmers for environmental, quality or animal welfare programmes through the reduction of direct payments for larger farms. Member states may choose to maintain a limited link between subsidy and production under well-defined conditions and within clear limits. See European Commission (2003a).

Figure 3.3 Share of EU agricultural spending on major member states 1992–2006 (%)

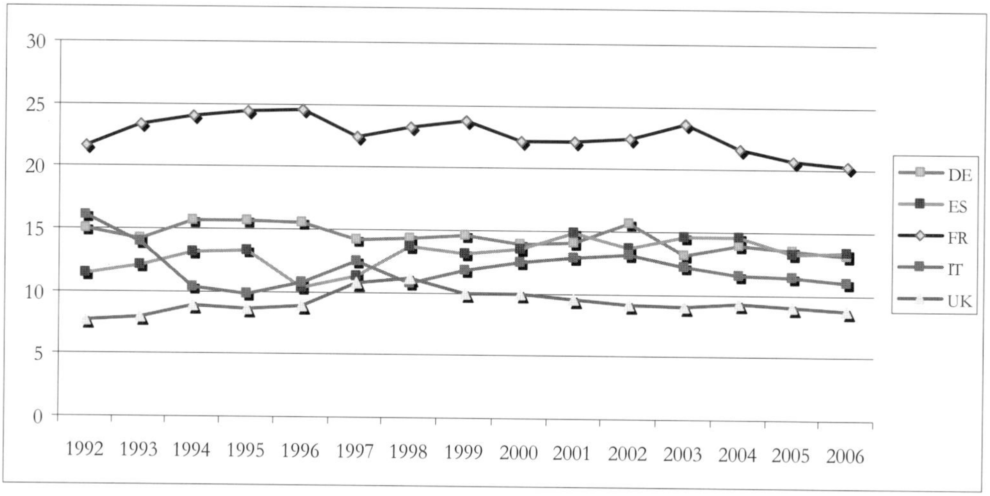

Source: Own calculations based on European Commission (2007l).

Agricultural spending in the UK takes a significant share. On average (see Table 3.4), agricultural spending constitutes 60% of EU expenditure on the UK. Only France shows a higher percentage (78%).

Table 3.4 Expenditure allocated to the major member states – Yearly average 1992–2006 (€ million)

	Germany	(%)	Spain	(%)	France	(%)	Italy	(%)	UK	(%)
Agriculture	5,796	58	5,309	44	9,111	78	4,838	55	3,740	60
Structural policies	3,386	34	6,478	54	2,014	17	3,344	38	1,874	30
Internal policies	757	8	287	2	614	5	563	7	644	10
Total	9,939	100	12,074	100	11,739	100	8,745	100	6,258	100

Source: Own calculations based on European Commission (2007l).

In the end, the only convincing and decisive argument for maintaining the UK rebate is the unanimity rule, which prevails for this kind of decision and the apparent political will of the UK to keep its contributions to the EU budget both as low as possible and as close as possible to the EU expenditure received. Figure 3.4 shows that this objective has been largely achieved thanks to the UK rebate. At the same time, Germany and Spain are, for different reasons, in a completely different situation.

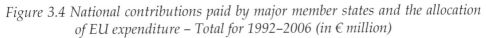

Figure 3.4 National contributions paid by major member states and the allocation of EU expenditure – Total for 1992–2006 (in € million)

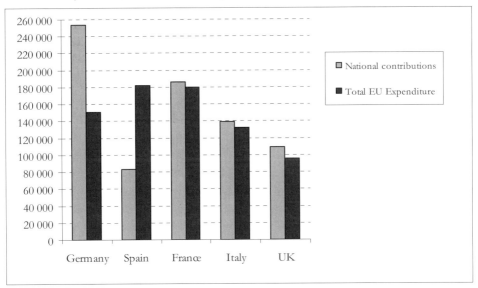

Source: Own calculations based on European Commission (2007l).

Concluding remarks

The UK's rebate is illustrative of the decision process in the context of the EU's finances. It represents one of the many arrangements negotiated in successive intergovernmental deals. Given the prevailing unanimity rule, there is little chance of discontinuing this rebate without introducing equivalent compensations for the UK and specific arrangements for other member states. It would be more logical in many respects if all member states were prepared to accept a single financing system, applied to all member states in the same way.

4. BUDGETARY BALANCES – AN IRRESISTIBLE TEMPTATION

Since the EU budget is largely financed through national contributions, member states feel justified in calculating the benefits accruing from it. The existence of the UK rebate and its calculation based on budgetary balances has established a practice that, moreover, draws support from an official methodology.[209] On this basis, data on member states' budgetary balances are regularly published by the Commission.

Hence, since they provide a balance between contributions paid by the member states and the payments they receive, budgetary balances conventionally represent the reference yardstick to define 'winners' and 'losers' in the framework of the EU budget. It is on this basis that the member states consider themselves (and are conventionally considered) net contributors or net beneficiaries. However undesirable it might be, the temptation "to try to strike a narrow arithmetical balance as to exactly how much day-to-day profit or loss each country is getting out of the Community" cannot be ignored.[210] Figure 4.1 shows the cumulative budgetary balances for the EU-15 member states for the period 1995–2006.

One should also observe (see Figure 4.2) that if EU expenditure may represent a significant amount in relation to GNI for some member states (Greece, Spain, Ireland and Portugal), the impact of the negative balance for net-payer member states is at most equal to 0.47% of their GNI.

---

[209] The principle of the calculation of budgetary balances is enshrined in the Own Resources Decision. The calculation method for the 2007–13 financial framework is provided for in a Commission Working Document presented to the Council of Ministers (see Adoption of a Council Decision on the system of the European Communities' own resources (EC, Euratom), Commission Working Document on calculation, financing, payment and entry in the budget of the correction of budgetary imbalances, 9851/07 ADD 2, Brussels, 23 May 2007(a)).

[210] See the speech by the then President of the European Commission Roy Jenkins to the European Parliament, 11 January 1977 (Jenkins, 1977).

Figure 4.1 EU-15 budgetary balances – Total for 1995–2006 (€ million)

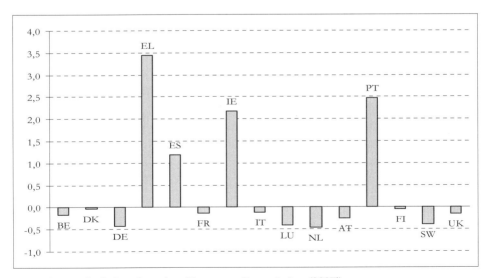

Source: Own calculations based on European Commission (2007l).

Figure 4.2 EU-15 budgetary balances as a share of GNI – Total for 1995–2006 (% of GNI)

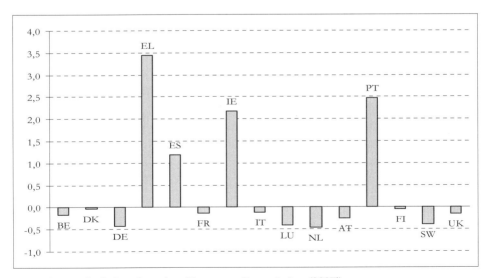

Source: Own calculations based on European Commission (2007l).

Estimating the benefits, a facile solution

As the Commission pointed out, budgetary balances "measured by the difference between contributions to and receipts from the EU budget, fail to account fully for the benefits accruing to member states from participating in the EU".[211] Notwithstanding the general acceptance that the balance of losses/gains of belonging to the EU cannot be captured by a single budgetary figure, such calculations have become a key element of the decision-making process of the Union.[212]

In addition, the method is based on the calculation of a balance between two sets of data that are conceptually different. While member states' contributions are financed through general taxation by all taxpayers, a similar parallelism does not exist for the payments made from the EU budget to a given country. The fact that EU expenditure is channelled predominantly into two main policies reduces at the same time the number

---

[211] See European Commission, *Budget Contributions, EU Expenditure, Budgetary Balances and Relative Prosperity of the Member States*, Paper presented by President Jacques Santer to the Ecofin Council, 13 October 1997(b). A full statement was made by the Commission in the 1998 own resources report (European Commission, 1998), chapter 2 and Annex 3. See also European Commission, *Proposal for a Council Decision on the system of the European Communities' own resources*, COM(2004) 501, Brussels, 3 August 2004(k), p. 2 and European Commission (Vol. II, 2004g), p. 17. A similar conclusion was drawn by the Court of Auditors: "Because of the integration of the member state economies within the single market, establishing a strict link between the destination of Community payments and the benefits accruing to the member states is becoming increasingly open to question" (see European Court of Auditors, 1998, para. 3.29). The European Council also "recognised that the full benefits of Union membership cannot be measured solely in budgetary terms" (see para. 68 of European Council, Presidency Conclusions of the Berlin European Council of 24-25 March, SN 100/1/99, Brussels, 1999). Finally, the European Parliament insisted "that the only possible solution is the abolition of the net balances system once and for all in parallel with a reform of the pattern of expenditure" (see European Parliament, Resolution of 29 March 2007, op. cit., para. 19).

[212] For example, in the framework of the 2007–13 financial perspective negotiations, the European Commission prepared the document "Calculating member states' net budgetary balances" for the European Council's Working Group on Own Resources (Brussels, 21 February 2005(f)), which presents different ways of calculating budgetary balances illustrated with quantitative estimates and a range of possible results.

of potential direct beneficiaries.[213] In terms of 'financial' flows these latter are substantially fewer than the taxpayers.

If the direct costs of the EU budget are easy to measure, the quantification of benefits is a different issue. The Commission has listed a series of reasons for which conventionally measured budgetary balances fail to represent the benefits of EU membership adequately, ending up with results that are not uncontroversial.[214] The concept of budgetary balances suffers from at least three main drawbacks:

- Budgetary balances fail to take account of positive externalities arising from EU policies as they benefit not only the immediate recipients but also give rise to spillover effects transcending national borders. Also, in areas such as research the level of expenditure does not adequately represent its impact in terms of growth and employment.

- EU budget expenditure is heterogeneous by nature. Agricultural, structural, research or administrative expenditures generate different spillover levels and a different added value for the recipient country. Owing to the diversity of circumstances and productive structures among member states, a given amount of EU expenditure will not result in the same economic benefits for all the member states.

- There are often difficulties associated with the identification of the ultimate beneficiaries of EU expenditure policies. CAP spending on export refunds is an example where expenditure may be recorded as allocated to the member state from which goods are exported when in fact the ultimate beneficiaries are the producers in other member states. Research expenditure, where the EU payment is made to one member of the consortium, also gives rise to similar difficulties.

The limited focus of the budgetary balances approach is shown for example by the link established between the Lisbon agenda and the structural funds. A substantial part of the 2007–13 appropriations will be used to contribute to the Lisbon growth and jobs objectives.[215] The Commission has observed that, "in a single market, those funds will be spent on procuring works, goods and services from all over the EU. That

---

[213] Among these are, for example, the almost 7 million EU farmers.

[214] See European Commission (1998), Annex 3.

[215] See footnote 67.

will benefit all member states and not just those directly receiving the most substantial amounts of structural funding."[216]

EU budget expenditure has indeed a role to play in raising the level of income in less developed areas and in making them more competitive. Raising the growth rate of these areas contributes definitively to the growth of the Union as such. Also, concerning specifically the impact of the enlargement on the EU-15 member state economies, several studies confirm that they will benefit to a greater extent from EU budget expenditure in relation to new member states.[217]

An indication is given in this respect by the trade balance of the new member states (EU-10) with the EU-15 as a whole. As shown in Table 4.1, the value of imports rose significantly after accession to the EU. In the period 2004–06, imports from the EU-15 increased on a yearly average by 56%, while exports to the EU-15 increased only by 38%. As a result, the negative trade balance for the period 2004–06 was considerably higher when compared with the period 2000–03. In contrast with the previous period, all EU-10 member states have recorded a negative trade balance with the EU-15 after accession.

---

[216] See European Commission, "Lisbon Strategy for Growth and Jobs: Frequently asked questions", Memo 06/474, Brussels, 8 December 2006(g).

[217] In European Parliament (2005a), the following studies are cited by Prof. Jedrzej Krakowski: European Commission, *Enlargement papers: The economic impact of enlargement*, DG for Economic and Financial Affairs, June 2001; F. Breuss, *Macroeconomic Effects of EU Enlargement for Old and New Members*, Working Paper No. 143, WIFO, Vienna, March 2001; P. Havlik, *EU Enlargement: Economic Impacts on Austria and the Five Acceding Central European Countries*, Research Reports No. 290, WIIW, Vienna, October 2002; C. Keuschnigg and W. Kohler, *Eastern Enlargement of the EU: Economic Costs and Benefits for the Present Member States?*, European Commission Study XIX/B1/9801, Brussels, September 1999; W. Quaiser, M. Hartman, E. Honekopp and M. Brendenmeier, *Die Osterweiterung der Europäischen Union: Konsequenzen für Wohlstand und Beschäftigung in Europa*, Friedrich Ebert Stiftung, Bonn, March 2000.

Table 4.1 Trade balance of EU-10 member states with the EU-15
– Total for 2000–03 and 2004–06 (€ billion)

Member states	2000–03			2004–06		
	Imports	Exports	Trade balance	Imports	Exports	Trade balance
Cyprus	8.33	3.61	-4.72	9.76	5.15	-4.61
Czech Republic	99.95	104.11	4.16	125.94	109.41	-16.53
Estonia	11.61	12.26	0.65	14.69	11.47	-3.23
Hungary	87.75	98.17	10.42	93.38	91.75	-1.63
Lithuania	12.83	10.49	-2.34	16.05	9.90	-6.15
Latvia	8.50	7.75	-0.75	9.73	8.39	-1.33
Malta	7.82	4.27	-3.55	6.37	3.25	-3.12
Poland	139.81	109.70	-30.12	163.82	124.21	-39.61
Slovenia	31.22	26.91	-4.31	34.74	23.51	-11.24
Slovakia	34.12	37.17	3.04	42.56	42.16	-0.39
Total	441.95	414.45	-27.50	517.04	429.21	-87.83
Yearly average	110.49	103.61	-6.88	172.35	143.07	-29.28

Source: Own calculations based on Eurostat data.

It is also interesting to note the relative situation concerning the main net-payer member states. Figure 4.3 compares the value of exports of these countries to EU-10 member states with the value of financial assistance that the EU-10 will receive during 2007–13 from the EU budget (for cohesion and rural development). The lower column in Figure 4.3 represents the pro rata of financing for net-payer member states (2007 budget). Two elements could be highlighted:

- In terms of value, the EU financial assistance planned during the next seven years represents around one fifth of the value of imports of the EU-10 from net-payer countries in the previous seven years. Moreover, as indicated earlier, the accession has increased the imports from the EU-15 and one could expect that this trend will continue in the future.

- Unsurprisingly, countries have not been performing in the same way. Some (for example, Germany and Italy) seem to have benefited from the EU-10 accession more than others. As observed earlier, member states have different productive structures and thus they record different results in relation to the economic consequences of the market enlargement.

Figure 4.3 Value of EU support for cohesion and rural development for EU-10 member states (2007–13) and their imports from net-payer member states, 2000–06 (€ million)

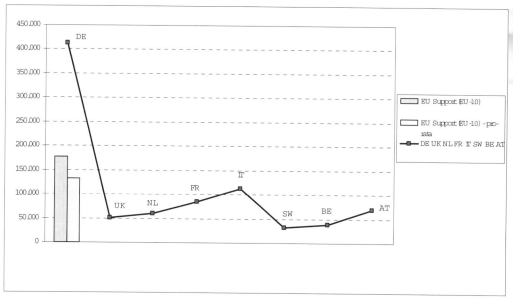

Source: Own calculations based on pre-allocated funding of the 2007–13 Financial Framework and Eurostat data.

The limited value of budgetary balances is also recognised at the national level, where one can assume that estimations of the potential economic benefit of EU expenditure is a current practice for national administrations. For example, the UK government highlights the positive impact for its economy derived from the enlargement.[218] Also, independent

---

[218] See the following extracts from the UK government's website http://www.fco.gov.uk:

Expanding the single market will have a profound effect on the economies of both new member states and existing members. It will provide new markets to exporters, and force prices down and increase choice for consumers across Europe.

studies were reported to indicate that the direct benefits of Agenda 2000 and enlargement for the UK would easily exceed £1 billion per year and that there would be, in addition, indirect benefits resulting from increased efficiency and competition and the development of new markets.[219]

Another example is given by the decision of the European Free Trade Association (EFTA) countries, i.e. Norway, Iceland and Lichtenstein as well as Switzerland, to contribute to the reduction of economic and social disparities in the member states that have recently joined the EU. Through the European Economic Area Financial Mechanism[220] and the Norwegian Financial Mechanism, Norway will make available €1.1 billion over the five-year period 2004–09, supporting investment and development programmes and projects in a wide range of priority sectors such as protection of the environment, conservation of the European cultural heritage, health and childcare and the development of human resources. A further €33 million will be provided by Iceland and Lichtenstein. In a similar context, Switzerland will provide around €650 million over five years (see Box 4.1).

UK merchandise trade with the new member states has increased by 392% since 1992, nearly 10 times as fast as with the rest of the world, and is steadily rising. There were around 14,000 UK firms exporting to Central and Eastern Europe in 2001. Firms like Tesco, Unilever, Vodafone, BP and International Power are successful investors in new member and candidate states.

New member states have adopted EU legislation on health and safety, the environment, consumer protection and state aids, meaning that UK investment is less risky, more transparent, and more competitive. The adoption of EU legislation means that in almost all areas, member states cannot discriminate between domestic businesses and those from other EU states.

[219] See House of Commons, Select Committee on Foreign Affairs, *Third Report*, Appendix 11, Supplementary Memorandum submitted by the Foreign and Commonwealth Office, London, 1999.

[220] This mechanism also funds investment projects in Greece, Portugal and Spain.

Box 4.1   Switzerland and EU cohesion policy

The Swiss financial assistance to Central and Eastern European countries was approved by referendum on 26 November 2006. It is interesting to note that among the arguments advanced by the Swiss government during the referendum to justify its financial assistance were the following points:

- On the basis of a study on the effects of public development aid, one franc of expenditure generates between 1.42 and 1.63 francs of GDP increase. The number of jobs generated is estimated to be between 13,000 and 19,000.*

- Since 1990, the financing of infrastructure in the Eastern European countries has generated orders for Swiss enterprises worth 780 million francs.

- Swiss development aid increases the possibilities for Swiss enterprises to obtain further orders.

The Swiss economy records huge commercial surpluses with the Eastern European countries (in 2005, 1.4 billion Swiss francs with the new EU-10 member states). Trade with these countries increases by about 10% each year and their economies record high growth rates.

* See Neumann et al. (2004) and Secrétariat d'Etat à l'économie SECO, Loi sur la coopération avec l'Europe de l'Est: Points principaux, October 2006.

Table 4.2 Trade balance of EFTA countries with EU-10 member states – Total for 2000–03 and 2004–06 (€ billion)

Countries	2000–03			2004–06		
	Imports	Exports	Trade balance	Imports	Exports	Trade balance
Total EFTA countries	13.1	16.1	3.0	15.4	12.1	-3.3
Switzerland	7.8	10.2	2.4	7.6	7.5	-0.1
Norway	4.8	5.6	0.8	7.1	4.3	-2.8

Source: Own calculations based on Eurostat data.

These contributions reflect the fact that these countries, through a multitude of bilateral agreements enjoy privileged access to the enlarged internal market and benefit from access to a number of EU programmes and activities. Although they are not EU members, their economies largely benefit from the development of the EU economy, even if, contrary to EU-15 member states, these countries record as a whole a trade deficit with EU-

10 member states after their accession to the EU. As Table 4.2 shows, this is mainly the case for Norway.

Concluding remarks

Despite being merely an accounting exercise that gives no reliable indication of the benefits of EU expenditure, above all on the economic impact for member states' economies, budgetary balances play a decisive role in EU finances. The 'negative balance' of the net-payer member states represents a limited fraction of their GNI, while it is assumed that their economies benefit from spillover effects derived from EU expenditure. For these reasons non-EU member states have decided to give financial support to the EU's cohesion policy. This move shows that while member states have a legitimate interest in assessing the benefits accruing from the EU budget, estimates should not be restricted to the 'budgetary balance' concept. Indeed, not only should citizens be made aware of the cost of the EU budget, they have also an interest in knowing the full benefits of EU expenditure in a meaningful way.

The 'betrayal' of Fontainebleau's ultimate goal

When introducing the UK rebate, the Fontainebleau European Council established the principle that "any member state sustaining a budgetary burden which is excessive in relation to its relative prosperity may benefit from a correction at the appropriate time".[221] The need for a rebate is examined on a case-by-case basis; there is no automatic mechanism that would allow other member states to qualify for a correction. Its application is founded on the agreement of the other member states, which consequently have to increase their own contributions correspondingly.[222] Despite specific requests by several member states,[223] the rebate has thus

---

[221] See European Council (1984).

[222] This means in practice a modification of the Own Resources Decision, which requires unanimity.

[223] In early 1998, Germany, Austria, Sweden and the Netherlands made such a request. The extension of the correction mechanism to other net contributors would have implied a huge – more than fourfold – increase of the rebates, from €2.9 billion (with the UK as the sole beneficiary) to €12.4 billion (with the UK and the other six member states), as it has been calculated by the European Court of Auditors (see European Court of Auditors, 1998, para. 3.27). See also European Commission (1998), p. 33.

been and still is being applied only in favour of the UK. Moreover, as member states benefiting from the rebate do not participate in its financing, a linear application of the UK rebate rules would imply that the burden of these huge rebates would have to be born by the less favoured member states. For this reason, other ways of reducing the financial burden of certain member states have been found.[224]

In an attempt to solve once and for all the issue of the budgetary burden, in 2004 the Commission proposed a generalisation of the correction mechanism, aimed at introducing a sort of safety net for large net contributors whose net contributions (calculated on the basis of the net budgetary balance) exceeded a certain level meant to represent the maximum accepted level of financial solidarity among member states (0.35% of a member state's GNI).[225] Net positions exceeding such a threshold would have been eligible for a correction (at a rate of 66%). Yet, the total refund volume was limited to a maximum of €7.5 billion a year, financed by all member states based on their relative share of GNI. According to a simulation, the UK was expected to receive €2.1 billion annually on average (raised to €3.1 billion thanks to transitional measures), against an average of €4.6 billion over the period 1997–2003.[226]

Unsurprisingly, "a broad spectrum of views [was] expressed"[227] by the member states on the Commission's proposal, which was finally not

---

[224] Among the solutions found are, for example, the gradual reduction of the weight of the VAT resource and the establishment and continuous increase of the GNI resource, a different share among member states for the financing of the UK rebate and ad hoc lump sums to some member states as decided for the financial perspective 2007–13. Also, the decision to increase, as of 2001, the share of traditional own resources retained by member states as 'collection costs' (from 10% to 25%) belongs to the category of ways of correcting excessive negative budgetary balances. See in this respect footnote 165.

[225] After examining the possibilities of reducing or phasing out the UK rebate, the Commission explored different parameters of a generalised correction mechanism, each having a different financial impact. This shows that what matters is actually not the conceptual design of the mechanism but rather finding an acceptable deal among member states, based on the financial impact for each of them in terms of contributions paid to the EU budget. See European Commission (Vol. II, 2004g), part II.6.

[226] See European Commission (Vol. II, 2004g), p. 40.

[227] See the Ecofin Council Conclusions (2004a), p. 9.

accepted. Indeed, in a context where the unanimity rule is required, why should the UK government have agreed to such a huge reduction of its rebate, some €4 billion per year less[228] compared with the mechanism rebate then applicable?

The Commission's proposal for a generalised correction mechanism calculated on the basis of the net budgetary balance of each member state in relation to the EU budget gives further credibility to a concept that fails to account fully for the benefits resulting from EU membership. The European Parliament has described generalising the rebate as a "double mistake since it would only strengthen the anti-communitarian character of the system and cement the short-sighted approach of a quantifiable 'juste retour'".[229] This stance taken by the Commission suggests that in making the best of a bad job, it has probably abandoned any hope that, as the Fontainebleau European Council established, "expenditure policy is ultimately the essential means of resolving the question of budgetary imbalances". It is worth recalling how far we are from the principles that the Commission tried to establish in the early years of the debate on the budgetary questions when it said that "the budget should not be judged in the light of the position of each member state, but mainly of the effectiveness with which it ensures the conduct of common policies to the benefit of the entire Community".[230] The Commission also said that "any solution must be found within the Community budget and must respect the integrity of the Community's system of own resources; its objective

---

[228] This figure takes into account the impact of the enlargement. See also footnote 160.

[229] See European Parliament, Resolution of 29 March 2007 (op. cit.), para. 19. The Court of Auditors has observed that the existence of any correction mechanism "compromises the simplicity and the transparency of the own resources system", as "calculating net balances implies numerous choices that must be made (on the items to be included, reference periods and accounting methods) all of which render any correction mechanism rather cumbersome". See European Court of Auditors, Opinion No. 4/2005 of 12 May 2005 on a proposal for a Council decision on the system of the European Communities' own resources and on a proposal for a Council Regulation on the implementing measures for the correction of budgetary imbalances in accordance with Articles 4 and 5 of the Council decision (...) on the system of the European Communities' own resources, OJ C 167, 7.7.2005, para. 19.

[230] See European Commission, *Reference paper on budgetary questions*, COM(79) 462, Brussels, 12 September 1979, p. 3.

must not be to put a member state in a position of juste retour in respect of the Community budget".[231]

Concluding remarks

The introduction of the UK rebate has been followed by other special arrangements on the revenue side for other member states. These arrangements have developed in view of finding an acceptable relationship for each member state between its disbursements to the EU budget and the expenditure it receives. As a result, the emphasis put on budgetary balances has overridden the intention of ultimately making EU expenditure the main tool for pursuing defined objectives.

Are there possible alternatives?

As the Commission had already pointed out in 1974, "it is very difficult to give a detailed view of the overall distribution of expenditure by country or by region, since it is not a matter of identifying the location of the direct recipient but rather of assessing the final economic impact".[232] Indeed, what matters is the final impact. The question, however, is whether there is any better system than budgetary balances to measure the impact of the EU budget.

In this respect, an attempt to assess the benefits of EU expenditure for the member states was made in a previous study,[233] which tried to overcome the conceptual weakness of the budgetary balances calculation by applying a macroeconomic analysis based on input–output tables and commercial trade flows. In this way, it was possible to estimate the increase in the demand for goods and services generated by EU expenditure. Quite unsurprisingly, the results, which are summarised in Figure 4.4, show that some member states that are at present considered 'net contributors' (for instance Belgium, Denmark, Germany, France, Italy, Austria and the UK) would actually appear as 'net recipients' if the increase in production from which they benefit was taken into account. Note the value of the real net

---

[231] See European Commission, Communication on Convergence and Budgetary Questions, COM(80) 147, Brussels, 20 March 1980, p. 1.

[232] See European Commission, "Inventory of the Community's economic and financial situation since enlargement and survey of future developments", *Supplement to Bulletin 7/74*, Brussels, 27 October 1974, p. 11.

[233] See Cipriani & Pisani (2004).

balance for Spain, which is more than two times higher than its budgetary balance, but also the fact that the Netherlands and Sweden remain net contributors in both scenarios.

Figure 4.4 Comparison of net balances (average 2000–02), EU-15 member states (€ million)

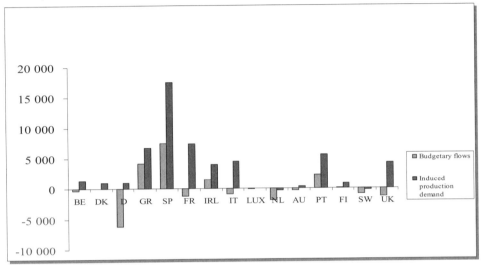

Source: Cipriani & Pisani (2004).

In order to highlight the change of place of each country in the hierarchy of net contributors, two rankings have been drawn up in Table 4.3. The first is based on budgetary flows (column *d*) and the second on induced demand (column *e*). Both rankings are arranged in descending order, placing in the 1st position the country most advantaged and in the 14th the largest net contributor. Compared with the budgetary flows ranking (column *d*), four countries improve their relative position if the induced demand is taken into account. In this way, France recovers nine positions, the UK six, Germany and Italy five each. Spain remains at the same level while all other member states would be given a lower ranking.

Independently of the degree of precision of the numerical results (very much dependent on the accuracy and the reliability of the available statistical data), it seems established that when evaluating the benefits accruing from European expenditure, the analysis of budgetary flows constitutes a very limited, and in a way misleading, instrument.

Table 4.3 Net balances according to budgetary flows and the induced demand, EU-15 member states (€ million, average 2000–02)

Member states	Net balance (€ million)		Ranking		
	Budgetary flows	Induced demand	Budgetary flows	Induced demand	Difference
a	b	c	d	e	f = d − e
Belgium	-299	1,364	7	8	-1
Denmark	-4	994	6	10	-4
Germany	-6,216	1,045	14	9	5
Greece	4,149	6,747	2	3	-1
Spain	7,504	17,552	1	1	0
France	-1,237	7,398	11	2	9
Ireland	1,531	4,043	4	7	-3
Italy	-894	4,497	10	5	5
Netherlands	-1,874	-331	13	14	-1
Austria	-345	381	8	12	-4
Portugal	2,253	5,574	3	4	-1
Finland	75	889	5	11	-6
Sweden	-863	-228	9	13	-4
UK	-1,270	4,221	12	6	6

Source: Cipriani & Pisani (2004).

The added value of an analysis based on the increase in domestic output generated by EU expenditure is that it discloses both the quantitative impact in the production of the EU expenditure and its geographical breadth. Actually, the 'real' balance is given by how much each member state economy really profits from EU expenditure. Indeed, as the analysis has shown, the same amount of EU expenditure in a given country can have a very different impact in the production of the beneficiary country (but also of the other countries benefiting from the induced demand), depending on the economic sector and because of the diversity of member states' industrial (and administrative) structures. The possibility of estimating both the quantitative and geographical effects of expenditure in a given country could give concrete implementation to the Fontainebleau European Council statement, according to which "expenditure policy is ultimately the essential means of resolving the question of budgetary imbalances".[234]

---

[234] See European Council (1984).

Moreover, it would even become possible to estimate the effects of a potentially different sectoral allocation of EU expenditure, taking into account the economic structure of each country. One would expect such concerns would also be at the heart of the "full, wide ranging review covering all aspects of EU spending, including the CAP"[235] asked for by the Council.

Concluding remarks

Without ignoring the difficulties associated with the establishment of a reliable and accepted way of estimating the benefits derived from EU expenditure, it seems clear that better alternatives to budgetary balances exist. The interest of taking advantage of these methodologies is not just their meaningfulness as such, but the fact that they could identify the impact by type of EU spending and highlight differences in the productive structures of the member states. The use of such instruments in the context of EU finances could enhance the guidance function of the EU budget, contribute to resolving any imbalances and increase the added value of EU expenditure.

---

[235] See European Council (2005a), para. 80.

5. RESPONSIBILITY, LOOKING FOR VOLUNTEERS

The EU budget is implemented through differentiated management methods (centralised management, shared or decentralised management and joint management), which are defined in the Financial Regulation.[236] Centralised management means that the Commission implements the budget either directly or through the agency of third parties. The shared or decentralised management concept implies that implementation tasks relating to the budget are delegated to member states or to third countries. In the event of joint management, certain implementation tasks are entrusted by the Commission to international organisations.

One of the characteristics of the EU budget is that almost all income and expenditure is managed by parties other than the Commission. The latter carries out, in a system of centralised management, only its own income and administrative expenditure,[237] some expenditure in the area of research and certain external actions. All the remaining appropriations (more than 80%) are disbursed either under shared management with the member states (own resources,[238] agricultural and structural policies)[239] or

---

[236] See Arts 53 to 57 of Council Regulation (EC, Euratom) No. 1605/2002 of 13 December 2006 (op. cit.).

[237] In the same way, each institution or Community body manages its own income and expenditure.

[238] The shared management concept is traditionally associated with expenditure. Own resources were included in this category by analogy, because national administrations are at the root of the fixing of the resources put at the disposal of the Communities to finance the budget.

[239] Apart from the fields mentioned, the different funds established in the framework of the migration flows policy (the external borders fund, the integration

under decentralised management with third countries (pre-accession aids) or are disbursed jointly with international organisations (humanitarian aid).

The choice of management method is a decision taken by the Council and binding on the Commission. Budgetary implementation under shared management is nothing other than the direct consequence of the principles of subsidiarity and proportionality. According to these principles, the Community intervenes only if (and insofar as) the objectives of the proposed action cannot be sufficiently achieved by the member states and can therefore be better achieved by the Community.[240]

Consequently, shared management also implies the absence of a genuine Community administration. The functions of authorising and validating income and expenditure decisions taken in Brussels are in the nature of formalities, authorising a use of the appropriations that has already been decided upon and thus allowing the authorising officer to implement measures, the substance of which is predetermined.[241] The implementation of the budget is hence no more than the utilisation of the appropriations; it does not include any genuine underlying decision, as is normally the case in national budgets. The decision-taking aspect is therefore dissociated from the financial implementation.

The shared management arrangements make member states responsible in the first instance, under the Commission's scrutiny, for the management, monitoring and day-to-day financial control of a large part of the present budget. At the same time, according to Art. 274 TEC, the Commission has final responsibility for the implementation of the EU budget. This system favours a lack of full accountability.[242]

---

fund, the return fund and the European refugee fund) are implemented under shared or decentralised management arrangements.

[240] See Art. 5 TEC. See also the section "The 'European' added value: What is it?".

[241] The reference here is to the multi-annual framework of the financial perspective. See the section "Financial perspective: Whose perspective?"

[242] Concerning the various aspects of responsibility in implementing the EU budget, see Cipriani (2006).

The need for a management culture

Since the early 1970s, as a result of the progressive development of common policies and successive enlargements, the need to adapt and improve the structures and procedures of the Commission's machinery has become more and more evident. Awareness of this has resulted in various internal and external studies and reports that have examined the functioning of the Commission's services and provided specific proposals for improvement.[243] But the recommendations presented in these reports have only been implemented to a limited extent.

The reform process received increased impetus towards the mid-1990s. At that time, the Commission was about to prepare the future financial framework beyond 2000, with the prospect of an enlarged Union and following far-reaching changes that had taken place over the previous decade (the accession of new member states, the modifications of the Treaties by the Single Act and the Treaty of Maastricht and two significant financial packages). The time was ripe to prepare future changes, not all the implications of which could be imagined.

The development of the EU required a greater focus than in the past on what was essential, giving priority to areas where the EU could provide real added value. To do that, it was necessary to promote the sound and efficient management of the Commission's services, by improving the use of human and financial resources and enhancing evaluation and monitoring. As evidence of the need for a deep change, above all in behaviour,[244] the then President of the European Commission Jacques

---

[243] In 1978, the Spierenburg Group was set up to examine ways of reforming the organisation, structures and administrative policy of the Commission. The Spierenburg report, published in 1979, called in particular for the appointment of a single vice president for coordinating the Commission's work and for a reduction in the number of Commissioners (one per member state), portfolios and directorates-general. Almost simultaneously three eminent politicians were asked to examine ways of improving the mechanisms and procedures of the Community institutions. The 'Report of the Three Wise Men', also submitted in 1979, confirmed many of the recommendations of the Spierenburg report.

[244] Concerning proper behaviour in the exercise of public office and the development of a consciousness for ethics in the functioning of EU institutions, see Giusta (2006).

Santer remarked, "My colleagues and I are determined to improve the Commission's budgetary and administrative culture."[245]

Against this background the Sound and Efficient Financial Management Programme (SEM 2000) was launched in 1995.[246] In 1997 a screening exercise was launched, known as 'Designing tomorrow's Commission' (Decode), with the aim of providing an up-to-date analysis of all activities carried out by the Commission, as well as the resources and working methods used, to enable it to plan its future and begin the process of reforming its organisation and the way it works.[247] During the same year, Agenda 2000 outlined the broad outlook for the development of the EU and its policies beyond the turn of the century, for the impact of enlargement on the Union as a whole and the future financial framework beyond 2000.[248]

Both SEM 2000 and Decode were combined in 1998 in a single measure, 'Tomorrow's Commission', seeking to change the Commission's management culture. During the same year, as a result of SEM 2000, 11

---

[245] See Santer (1995).

[246] The first two stages of the initiative concerned management reforms within the Commission itself, resulting in three communications in 1995 setting out a programme of action. The third stage concerned improved partnership with the member states on the financial management of EU expenditure; it involved the creation, in 1996, of a group of personal representatives of finance and budget ministers who mainly dealt with the management of the structural policies. One of the main results of this exercise was the adoption of Commission Regulation (EC) No. 2064/97 of 15 October 1997 establishing detailed arrangements for the implementation of Council Regulation (EEC) No. 4253/88, OJ L 290, 23.10.1997, which sets down minimum standards of financial control by the member states of operations co-financed by the structural funds. SEM 2000 was also at the origin of the MAP 2000 programme, built around a threefold strategy (decentralisation, simplification and personnel management) and aimed at in-depth changes in the field of administration and personnel policy.

[247] The final report formulated a number of recommendations on the organisation and running of the Commission in different areas, including performance indicators, internal coordination, good practices and control.

[248] For a description of Agenda 2000, see footnote 42.

recommendations were presented.[249] Also in 1998, the Williamson report on the modernisation of staff policy was presented.

All these initiatives witnessed the acknowledgment that to cope with future challenges the Commission's budgetary and administrative culture would have to be radically changed at all levels. Hence, the objective was ambitious, covering at the same time improving effectiveness and supervision in the management of funds, monitoring the execution of decentralised tasks and increasing institutional and staff accountability. Indeed, "the Commission has had to take on a growing number of new tasks, resulting in successive reorganisations which have often had to be carried out hastily and without adequate preparation".[250]

A profound change in the working culture of the Commission would have meant transforming a classical international organisation of generalists into a modern administration of policy managers, capable of managing an increased amount of funds in various policy areas within a unique institutional framework. It must be recognised that the task was not easy as the Commission was trying to undertake by way of reform in a few years more than it had done in the previous 40 years.

The year 1998 marked a watershed in the reform process, with the European Parliament first postponing and then refusing to give discharge to the Commission for the 1996 financial year,[251] thus making official the

---

[249] Among these were the following: Recommendation No. 2 – whenever policy decisions are taken, establish the full cost of any proposal in terms of financial, human and other resources (link between the administrative appropriations and operating appropriations); Recommendation No. 4 – systematic evaluation for all Community programmes and action; DG XIX and XX to step up their work on improving cost-effectiveness and evaluation techniques; and Recommendation No. 7 – departments to ensure, when drafting a regulation and at subsequent stages ending with final adoption, that it is clear and amenable to control and contains safeguards against attempted fraud.

[250] See European Commission (1997a), p. 48.

[251] See European Parliament, Resolution of 31 March 1998 (op. cit.) and the Minutes of 17 December 1998. This was the second time discharge was refused. It had occurred previously in November 1984 concerning the 1982 financial year. Ironically, the Commission's President was another Luxembourger, Gaston Thorn, who did not resign, however, as the term of office of the Commission was to expire only few weeks afterwards.

crisis of the EU's financial management. One year later, the Parliament highlighted "the Commission's belated recognition of the crisis facing it regarding the financial management of the Community budget and its lack of transparency and accountability" and finally called for a Committee of Independent Experts to "examine the way in which the Commission detects and deals with fraud, mismanagement and nepotism, including a fundamental review of Commission practices in the awarding of all financial contracts".[252]

The Committee of Independent Experts provided two reports[253] in which they found more particularly that the administrative and financial culture, the sense of individual responsibility among staff and awareness of the need to comply with the rules of sound financial management had not developed with the progressive assignment of implementation tasks to the Commission. The Committee noted at the same time a mismatch between the objectives assigned to the Commission and the resources that the Commission was able or chose to employ. It found no evidence of any attempt by the Commission to assess in advance the volume of resources required when a new policy was discussed among the Community institutions. The Committee also expressed concern at the growing reluctance among the members of the hierarchy to acknowledge their responsibility:

> It is becoming difficult to find anyone who has even the slightest sense of responsibility. However, that sense of responsibility is essential. It must be demonstrated, first and foremost, by the Commissioners individually and the Commission as a body. The temptation to deprive

---

[252] See European Parliament, Resolution of 14 January 1999 on improving the financial management of the Commission, para 1. See also the Resolution of 23 March 1999 on the resignation of the Commission and the appointment of a new Commission.

[253] See Committee of Independent Experts, *First Report on Allegations Regarding Fraud, Mismanagement and Nepotism in the European Commission*, Brussels, 15 March 1999(a). The Committee's *Second Report on Reform of the Commission: Analysis of current practice and proposals for tackling mismanagement, irregularities and fraud* was published on 10 September 1999(b). Mr Walter van Gerven, who has been member of the Experts Committee, has defined the first sentence of the quotation as a *'cri du coeur'*, an overstatement that could have been omitted. See van Gerven (2007), p. 7.

the concept of responsibility of all substance is a dangerous one. That concept is the ultimate manifestation of democracy.[254]

The Committee finally observed that the Community civil service "tends to favour planning and negotiation at the expense of management and monitoring, which are less highly thought of" and prefers "to think rather than to do".[255]

It was not sufficient for the Santer Commission to adopt, in the first months of 1999, two codes laying down the rules of conduct and organisation applicable to Members of the Commission and governing the relations between Commissioners and Commission departments.[256] The Santer Commission resigned in March 1999, under the threat of a censure motion, immediately after publication of the first report of the Committee of Independent Experts.

The Committee's reports (and the subsequent resignation of the Commission) gave rise to serious concerns and a fall in motivation among the Commission staff, at all levels. The general feeling was that staff were being held unjustly responsible for the somewhat unorganised growth of the Commission's tasks.[257]

In 2000, the "revolution in the Commission's operating procedures"[258] materialised in a White Paper on Reform.[259] Meant to be "a real

---

[254] See Committee of Independent Experts (1999a), para. 9.4.25.

[255] See Committee of Independent Experts (1999b), para. 8.3.

[256] Later in the year, a code of ethics for officials was also introduced.

[257] Maybe because it was aware of this feeling, the Committee of Independent Experts recognised in its second report that they "had the opportunity of meeting many Commission officials of widely differing levels of seniority and doing a great variety of jobs. In most cases the Committee was appreciative of their abilities, their spirit of public service and their sincere desire to play their part in the efforts needed to improve the system." See Committee of Independent Experts (1999b), para. 8.4.

[258] See the address delivered by Romano Prodi (1999) to the European Parliament of 21 July 1999.

[259] See European Commission, White Paper on Reforming the Commission, COM(2000) 200, Brussels, 1 March 2000. The Commission intended to turn over a new leaf and to break completely with the past. More specifically, the declared objective was to embed in the Commission's administrative culture the need to improve the quality, relevance and definition of objectives and indicators, and to

organisational and cultural Big Bang",[260] the main aim was once again to put in place an administrative structure suited in all respects to dealing with the expanded role and competencies of the EU.

Since 2000, many actions have been implemented to achieve greater efficiency and accountability. Roadmaps[261] and action plans have become a recurrent practice, as well as the extensive use of reporting initiatives. The Commission's services have undergone sometimes profound

---

report on performance. 'Activity-based management' was introduced to establish the relationships between objectives, actions and resources. To make the best possible use of human resources, measures were proposed to favour a greater degree of meritocracy, more credible and verifiable performance appraisal, lifelong learning and devolved management responsibility. In addition, a new system aiming at combining the decentralisation of management control with an effective central audit system was introduced to improve financial management (for a progress report on the Commission's reform, see European Commission, Communication on a Progress report on the Commission reform beyond the reform mandate, COM(2005) 668, Brussels, 21 December 2005(g)).

[260] See the speech by Romano Prodi (2000b) to the European Parliament of 1 March 2000.

[261] For example, following the repeated qualification of the Court of Auditors' yearly statement on the legality/regularity of EU spending, namely in the large expenditure areas of the agricultural and structural policies, in 2005 the Commission launched a Communication on a roadmap to an integrated internal control framework (see European Commission, COM(2005) 252, Brussels, 15 June 2005(h)). This has been followed by a panel of member states' experts, by the establishment of a 'gap assessment' of the Commission's services (see European Commission, *A gap assessment between the internal control framework in the Commission Services, and the control principles set out in the Court of Auditors' "proposal for a Community internal control framework" Opinion No. 2/2004*, Commission Staff Working Document, SEC(2005) 1152, Brussels, 28 September 2005(i)) and finally by an action plan currently under implementation (see European Commission, Communication on a Commission Action Plan towards an Integrated Internal Control Framework, COM(2006) 9, Brussels, 17 January 2006(h)). In its 2006 Annual Report, the Court of Auditors found that the impact of the Commission's action plan "is only likely to be evident in the medium to long term" (para. 0.8) and that, at the end of 2006, the large majority of these actions were still in progress or required follow-up as the objective was not entirely achieved or the impact was not yet realised (2007c, para. 2.22).

reorganisations, audit staff have been increased and their accountability enhanced, especially with the reporting obligations of directors-general.[262] The staff culture of the European Commission has changed considerably.

It remains a fact, however, that the Commission, as an institution, has not necessarily evolved in one key aspect: assuming full responsibility for the implementation of the EU budget. The European Parliament and the Court of Auditors[263] were quick to point out that the increased responsibility of directors-general was not accompanied by the endorsement of direct (and not only political) responsibility by the Members of the Commission.[264]

---

[262] According to the Financial Regulation (Art. 60(7)), each director-general is to report to his/her institution on the performance of his/her duties in the form of an annual activity report together with financial and management information confirming that the information contained in the report presents a true and fair view except as otherwise specified in any reservations related to defined areas of revenue and expenditure. The report must indicate the results of the operations by reference to the objectives set, the risks associated with these operations, the use made of the resources provided and the efficiency and effectiveness of the internal control system.

[263] See the European Parliament, Resolution of 12 April 2005 on the discharge for implementation of the European Union general budget for the financial year 2003 (para. 62). See also Resolution of 27 April 2006 on the discharge for implementation of the European Union general budget for the financial year 2004 (paras 74 to 80) and the Resolution of 24 April 2007 for the financial year 2005 (op. cit., paras 71 to 73). In this last Resolution, the Parliament referred to the opinion expressed by the Commission's internal auditor to the effect that "a full involvement of Commissioners to evaluate political risks would allow better overall management of risks and thus improve planning, resource allocation and policy delivery" (para. 72). The Parliament even went on to insist that "with some exceptions, Commissioners need to be better prepared for hearings concerning the 2006 discharge procedure" (para. 74). For the European Court of Auditors, see the *Annual Report concerning the financial year 2004* (European Court of Auditors, 2005), para. 1.57.

[264] As in 2005, in the synthesis of management achievements in 2006, the Commission made this declaration: "By adopting this synthesis, the Commission assumes its political responsibility for management by its Directors-General and Heads of service, on the basis of the assurances and reservations made by them in these Reports, while acknowledging that further efforts are needed to resolve a number of weaknesses." See European Commission (2007d), p. 2. The Commission

Concluding remarks

The staff culture – it could not be otherwise – is very much dependent upon the strategic role that the institution attributes to itself. As the European Parliament observed, "internal control in the Commission will never be stronger than the political will behind it".[265]

Are shared management and accountability compatible?

Convinced that its responsibility as regards the implementation of the budget is broader than its executive powers, the Commission has repeatedly shown that it is reluctant to accept full responsibility for the execution of a budget that is largely predetermined and managed by the member states and their administrations. In 1987, at a time when the EU budget was gradually increasing assistance for structural policies, the Commission had already held that its "responsibility for monitoring implementation will be reduced since the member states will be involved more directly in the management" of the programmes.[266] In the 2000 White Paper on Reform, the Commission developed the policy of externalising the implementation tasks for certain programmes to executive agencies, with

---

points out that the "2000 reform centred on ensuring Authorising Officers by Delegation were solely responsible for the execution of their activities", hence Commissioners "could not be further involved in the management of the risks without going against the separation of tasks and responsibilities between Commissioners and Directors-general" (see European Commission, *Report from the Commission to the European Parliament on the follow-up to 2005 discharge decisions (summary)*, COM(2007) 538, Brussels, 19 September 2007(r), p. 6, and the attached Commission Working Document, SEC(2007) 1185, p. 17). This stance does not seem to be in line with the logic of the delegation of tasks set in the Financial Regulation. Indeed, the Commission is the 'authorising officer' and directors-general are authorising officers by delegation of the Commission. According to the general principles of Community law, only tasks can be delegated, not the responsibility. For example, in the event of subdelegation, the authorising officer by delegation continues to be responsible for the efficiency and effectiveness of the internal management and control systems put in place and for the choice of the authorising officer by subdelegation (see the Financial Regulation, Arts 59, 60 and 66).

[265] See European Parliament, Resolution of 27 April 2006 (op. cit.), para. 78.

[266] See European Commission (1987), p. 21.

the objective of focusing Commission staff resources on the institution's core tasks of achieving the goals of Community programmes more effectively.[267] This stance was further confirmed by the proposal in the 2007–13 financial perspective.[268]

The Commission has interpreted the concept of responsibility as basically limited to the implementation of the specific tasks that it considers its personal duty and tends to dissociate its own responsibilities from those

---

[267] See European Commission (2000). Executive agencies are the central element of the new externalisation instrument. They are created by the Commission, which supervises the steering committee of the agency, and are directly responsible for the implementation of specific Community programmes. Four executive agencies have so far been created: the Executive Agency for Competitiveness and Innovation (previously the Intelligent Energy Executive Agency), the Public Health Executive Agency, the Education, Audiovisual and Culture Executive Agency and the Trans-European Transport Network Executive Agency. Others are on their way, such as two or more for the implementation of parts of the 7th Research Framework Programme. It is worth noting that the European Parliament recently considered that the "ever growing number of Agencies does not always reflect the real needs of the Union and its citizens" and therefore invited the Commission "to present a cost-benefit study before the setting up of any new Agency" (see European Parliament, Resolution of 24 April 2007, op. cit., para. 180). In the same Resolution, the Parliament also underlined the need for a cost-benefit analysis, which, for example, was not satisfactory in the case of the externalisation of the management of Community financial support for the trans-European transport network (see para. 203). In this respect, the Interinstitutional Agreement for the 2007–13 financial framework foresees that

> when drawing up its proposal for the creation of any new agency, the Commission will assess the budgetary implications for the expenditure heading concerned. On the basis of that information and without prejudice to the legislative procedures governing the setting up of the agency, the two arms of the budgetary authority commit themselves, in the framework of budgetary cooperation, to arrive at a timely agreement on the financing of the agency. (European Parliament, Council and Commission, 2006, para. 47)

[268] The proposal states, "one of the fundamental principles of Commission reform is that the Commission's core administration will in future focus on the development and monitoring of policies under the Treaty. The execution of these policies, as well as other executive activities at a European level, will where appropriate be delegated to other bodies." See European Commission (2004a), Annex 1, p. 39.

that are specifically devolved to the member states.[269] As a consequence, the Commission and the member states are to a large extent more 'counterparts' than partners. Proof of this way of thinking is, for example, the legislative reform of the structural funds, where one of the main goals was meant to "clearly delimit...the framework, the nature, and the division of responsibility between the different actors concerned by the execution of the Community budget".[270] The Commission's proposal to amend Art. 274

---

[269] This concept seems to have recently met with some degree of sympathy at the European Parliament, whose position has evolved somewhat in recent years. In 2004, the Parliament stressed that, "even though the day-to-day management is shared, financial responsibility remains indivisible and ultimate responsibility for implementation lies with the Commission" (see European Parliament, Resolution of 21 April 2004 on the discharge for implementation of the European Union general budget for the financial year 2002, para. 8). It repeated the same concept in 2005 (see the Resolution of 12 April 2005, op. cit., para. 19). The Parliament's position changed in 2006 when it emphasised that "the overriding principle advocated by Parliament is that the relevant political authorities within the member states take full responsibility for the funds placed at their disposal" (see European Parliament, Resolution of 2 February 2006 on national management declarations, para. 9). One may observe that this same concept was mentioned in the 2004 Discharge Resolution, omitting however the reference to the 'full' responsibility of the member states for the funds placed at their disposal (see the Resolution of 27 April 2006, op. cit., para. H). The Parliament finally determined in 2007 "that each member state must be able to take responsibility for the management of EU funds received" (see European Parliament, Resolution of 24 April 2007, op. cit., para. 23).

[270] See European Commission, *Proposal for a Council Regulation laying down general provisions on the European Regional Development Fund, the European Social Fund and the Cohesion Fund*, COM(2004) 492, Brussels, 14 July 2004(l), para. 5.3. Council Regulation (EC) No. 1083/2006 of 11 November 2006 (op. cit.) specifies the respective responsibilities of the Commission and the member states (see Arts 70 to 73). For example, following the Commission's proposal and in contrast with the rules applicable to the previous financial perspective (see Art. 35(2) of Council Regulation (EC) No. 1260/1999, OJ L 161, 26.6.1999), the Regulation does not foresee a systematic participation of the Commission in the 'monitoring committees' (see Art. 64(2)). These committees are nevertheless in charge of assessing the effectiveness and quality of the implementation of operational programmes financed by the structural funds, by reviewing progress made towards achieving the specific targets and proposing suitable measures.

TEC in the framework of the European Convention[271] is another confirmation of this principle of management separation.

The process of progressively shifting the Commission's management responsibilities to third bodies, although often justified on the grounds of the 'smart' objective of simplification, has found further recognition in the recent amendments of the financial rules. The Financial Regulation has confirmed that the implementing tasks delegated by the Commission "must be clearly defined and fully supervised as to the use made of them",[272] thus requiring the Commission to make sure that all the conditions necessary for such a delegation are met (in practice, that the national management and control systems work properly). But the amended provisions have given an extensive interpretation of the concept of delegation, enhancing the responsibility of member states in the event of shared management. The Commission's role of ensuring that the funds are

---

[271] The Commission called on the Convention "to examine the feasibility of sharing responsibility for budget implementation when the member states are responsible for most of the management of funds" (see European Commission, Communication on a Project for the European Union, COM(2002) 247 final, Brussels, 22 May 2002(d), p. 6). The Commission representatives to the European Convention also proposed, although unsuccessfully, that member states take part, along with the Commission, in the procedure of auditing the accounts for the discharge. Thus, the annual report of the Court of Auditors would have been accompanied by the answers of all member states. The European Parliament could also have asked to hear the member states, which could even have been the subject of observations sent to them directly (see European Convention, Proposal for an amendment to Art. III-311 of the draft Treaty submitted by Messrs Barnier, Vitorino, O'Sullivan and Ponzano, 2003(d), retrieved from **http://european-convention.eu.int/docs/treaty/pdf/892/Art%20III%20311%20Barnier%20FR.pdf**). Currently, pursuant to the Financial Regulation (Art. 143(6)), member states forward their comments to the Commission, which draws up a report for this purpose. In the report concerning the financial year 2002 the Commission reiterated its wish to include the member states in the contradictory procedure with the Court of Auditors so they could defend their point of view directly (see European Commission, *Report from the Commission on Member States' replies to the Court of Auditors' 2002 Annual Report*, COM(2004) 859, Brussels, 5 January 2005(j), p. 14).

[272] See Art. 54(1) of Council Regulation (EC, Euratom) No. 1605/2002 of 13 December 2006 (op. cit.).

used in accordance with the applicable rules is focused on financial correction mechanisms that "enable it to assume final responsibility for the implementation of the budget".[273] (See also Box 5.1).

Box 5.1 Financial corrections

For different reasons, reliance cannot be put solely on financial corrections to guarantee a correct implementation of the EU budget. Because they are likely to lead to legal disputes, financial corrections often generate long drawn-out procedures, the outcome of which is uncertain. In addition, the amount of the financial corrections appears to be in practice not particularly high (around 0.5% in agricultural and structural policies), so it is not possible to argue that the financial corrections have a key dissuasive effect. Also, financial corrections do not constitute genuine financial sanctions. They essentially represent the recovery of irregular expenditure, the impact of which is often neutralised by the replacement of one project by another, as happens in the case of the structural funds. In addition, the cost is generally borne by the member states and not by the final recipients. In this perspective, they constitute a further contribution by taxpayers. The practical possibility of imposing financial corrections is also limited by the necessarily reduced number of the Commission's controls, which, moreover, generally occur at the end of a programme, i.e. at a stage where, despite any potential financial correction, it is no longer possible to correct fundamental system weaknesses and re-direct the objectives to be achieved by the co-financed policies. Finally, by their very nature, financial corrections can be applied only in the event of the established violation of precise rules. They are therefore much more suitable for sanctioning violations of legality and regularity rather than weaknesses in terms of sound financial management.

---

[273] Ibid., Art. 53b(4). While expressing "grave concern at the large number of errors detected by the Court in transactions at final beneficiary level", the European Parliament noted "where there is a shared management arrangement, responsibility for preventing, identifying and correcting errors at final beneficiary level lies with the member states whilst at the same time the Commission is responsible for giving clear, efficient and effective guidelines to member states on how to prevent, identify and correct these errors". In the case where member states' control systems are still insufficient the Parliament called on the Commission to "impose clear deadlines and apply sanctions where those deadlines are not met" (see European Parliament, Resolution of 24 April 2007, op. cit., paras 14–15).

Box 5.1, cont.

Observance of the latter principle is however a key element of the conditions on which the implementation of the budget should be based. For all these reasons the Commission's confidence in the capacity of this instrument to ensure observance of the applicable provisions, thus making good any loss to the Community's budget, does not meet with unanimous agreement. The European Parliament wondered for example "if the current system of financial correction is sufficient to encourage member states to combat fraud and irregularities".* The Court of Auditors remarked that the financial corrections could provide no more "than a limited, auxiliary contribution to the necessary rigour of everyday management. Their effectiveness is essentially dependent on the number of checks performed. Furthermore, since financial corrections would intervene only after the fact, they could not be enough on their own to make good all the consequences of any transactions that might be implemented even though they did not meet the necessary regulatory requirements."**

---

* See European Parliament, Resolution of 10 April 2002 on the discharge for implementing the general budget of the European Union for the financial year 2000, para. 78.

** See European Court of Auditors, Opinion No. 2/2005 of 18 March 2005 on the proposal for a Council Regulation laying down general provisions on the European Regional Development Fund, the European Social Fund and the Cohesion Fund, OJ C 121, 20.5.2005, para. 14.

It is worth noting that a recent amendment to the Commission's rules implementing the Financial Regulation omitted the previous provision whereby in the event of shared management, the Commission "shall first carry out document and on-the-spot checks into the existence, relevance and proper operation within the entities to which it entrusts implementation, in accordance with the rules of sound financial management" of the procedures applied, of control systems, of accounting systems and procurement and grant award procedures.[274]

---

[274] See Art. 35(1) of Commission Regulation No. 2342/2002 of 23 December 2002 laying down detailed rules for the implementation of Council Regulation (EC, Euratom) No. 1605/2002 on the Financial Regulation applicable to the general

This means that in practice, the setting-up and the management of the programmes implemented in shared management arrangements are left fully in the hands of the member states. The supervisory role of the Commission is limited to issuing manuals and notes on best practice, which, however detailed, cannot be imposed (because of the subsidiarity principle) on the thousands of national bodies that are not directly or functionally subordinated to it. Incidentally, the Commission also carries out, to the extent possible, some controls that are limited in number and in impact. Its services acknowledge that they are unable to check systematically the reliability of information on the numerous national systems, especially as regards the structural policies.[275] The European

---

budget of the European Communities (OJ L 357, 31.12.2002). This provision is no longer applicable since Commission Regulation (EC, Euratom) No. 478/2007 of 23 April 2007 amending Regulation (EC, Euratom) No. 2342/2002 laying down detailed rules for the implementation of Council Regulation (EC, Euratom) No. 1605/2002 on the Financial Regulation applicable to the general budget of the European Communities (OJ L 111/13, 28.4.2007). The low implementation rate for the structural funds (see the section "Is the size of the budget a major issue?" and footnote 29 in particular) is symptomatic of the necessity to make sure beforehand that national systems can effectively cope with the different requirements and the volume of funds attributed. A study undertaken for the European Parliament investigated the main reasons limiting the effective implementation of structural funds in Poland. According to the study, the implementation of the structural funds suffered from deficiencies in terms of establishing the necessary legal, organisational and human resources framework to enable the effective use of support. To ensure a proper implementation during the 2007–13 period, the study concluded that the legal framework needs to be finalised, access to co-financing should be made easier, a close monitoring of the implementation should be made certain and, finally, staff training should be organised, in particular on public procurement and environmental legislation (see European Parliament, *The Structural Funds' Implementation in Poland – Challenges for 2007-2013*, Budgetary Affairs, September 2007(b)).

[275] See European Commission, Communication on Synthesis of 2003 Annual Activity Reports of DGs and Services, COM(2004) 418 final, Brussels, 19 July 2004(m), p. 8. The assessment of the effective functioning of national systems undertaken by the directorates-general responsible for structural policies indicate that the majority of the funds are managed by national systems in need of

Parliament has nonetheless asked the Commission to "present every six months a scoreboard showing member states' progress as regards efficient implementation of supervisory and control systems as described in the regulations".[276]

---

improvements to correct material deficiencies in key controls and, in some cases, by seriously deficient systems.

[276] See European Parliament, Resolution of 27 April 2006 (op. cit.), para. 135. The Interinstitutional Agreement for the 2007–13 period also provides,

> As part of their enhanced responsibilities for structural funds and in accordance with national constitutional requirements, the relevant audit authorities in member states will produce an assessment concerning the compliance of management and control systems with the regulations of the Community. Member states therefore undertake to produce an annual summary at the appropriate national level of the available audits and declarations. (European Parliament, Council and Commission, 2006, para. 44)

This is confirmed by the Financial Regulation (see Art. 53b(4) of Council Regulation (EC, Euratom) No. 1605/2002 of 13 December 2006, op. cit.). The modalities of this assessment by the relevant national audit authorities concerning the compliance of management and control systems for the structural funds are provided for in Art. 62(1) of Council Regulation (EC) No. 1083/2006 of 11 November 2006, op. cit.). The European Parliament has expressed confidence that this assessment of the audit authorities "should make a substantial contribution towards improving management of the Community budget", and has asked the Commission "to draw up, on the basis of that information, a document analysing the strengths and weaknesses of each member state's national system for the administration and control of Community funds and the results of the audits conducted" (see European Parliament, Resolution of 24 April 2007, op. cit., paras E and 34). In the light of the important role played by the member states in budgetary implementation, the European Parliament previously suggested that each minister for finance draw up "an annual ex-post Declaration of Assurance as regards the legality and regularity of the underlying transactions" (see European Parliament, Resolution of 12 April 2005, op. cit., para. 21). This suggestion, however, was not favourably received by the member states, with the Council of Ministers invoking the need "not to put into question the existing balance between the Commission and the member states or to compromise responsibility and accountability at the operational level" (see the Ecofin Council Conclusions, 13678/05, Brussels, 8 November 2005, p. 9). Nonetheless, some member states have expressed the intention of proceeding in that direction on a voluntary basis (for example, Denmark, the Netherlands, Sweden and the UK).

If shared management has developed de facto into two distinct levels of management, the 'solution' towards accountability has been found in a tightly-woven system of declarations, to be produced by the relevant national bodies with a view to certifying the compliance of the operations financed by the EU budget with the rules applicable. This has especially been the case since 1995, when the Court of Auditors established for the first time a yearly statement of assurance on EU expenditure.[277] Because of the level of errors found, the Court has never been able to deliver an unqualified statement concerning expenditure under shared management.[278] The Barroso Commission has made a strategic objective out of obtaining an unqualified statement of assurance from the Court.[279] The Commission expects to derive assurance from this system of declarations and thus to be confident that the expenditure it authorises will prove in the end to be in full compliance with the applicable rules.

---

[277] Art. 248 TEC, as modified by the Maastricht Treaty, stipulates that the Court of Auditors "shall provide the European Parliament and the Council with a statement of assurance as to the reliability of the accounts and the legality and regularity of the underlying transactions". The main objectives are to inform the discharge authority of whether

- the consolidated financial statements of the general budget of the European Union, as drawn up by the European Commission, present a true and fair view of the financial activities for the year and of the year-end situation; and

- legal and contractual provisions have been respected when executing the budget.

[278] Although the Court has recently recognised, concerning agricultural spending, that "where properly applied", the "Integrated Administration and Control System…is an effective control system for limiting the risk of error or irregular expenditure" (see European Court of Auditors, 2006a, para. 5.53). It is worth noting that the Court has issued a qualified statement also for areas where the Commission has a direct management responsibility, such as in the case of research spending. It should also be observed that despite the continuous qualified statements by the Court on the legality of expenditure, the European Parliament has not, for all that, refused to give discharge to the Commission or demanded its resignation by a censure vote (ex Art. 201 TEC).

[279] See European Commission, Communication from the President in agreement with Vice-President Wallström, Strategic Objectives 2005–2009, Europe 2010: A Partnership for European Renewal, Prosperity, Solidarity and Security, COM(2005) 12 final, Brussels, 26 January 2005(k), p. 5. See also footnote 261.

It seems clear that the responsibility itself cannot be delegated,[280] all the more so because member states do not seem prepared to accept it in place of the Commission. The question is therefore how this cascade of declarations will allow in practice for full accountability, knowing, for example, that the Commission is not willing to take a position, on an annual basis, on the legality of the expenditure incurred by the member states, but rather prefers to wait (because of the multi-annual nature of the programming period) for the closure of the programming period, hence putting absolute confidence in the 'thaumaturgic' effect of financial corrections, which nonetheless remains to be proved.[281] The European Court of Auditors has just made this observation: "A declaration that systems are functioning as required by EU regulations may not in itself provide assurance about the legality and regularity of the transactions concerned."[282] The risk is that, on the contrary, a fundamental gap in the chain of financial responsibility will remain and will result, in the end, in a de facto amendment of the provisions of Art. 274 TEC, according to which the Commission "shall implement the budget...having regard to the principles of sound financial management".[283]

---

[280] One could not state this principle more solemnly than by referring to the Financial Regulation: "The implementation methods should guarantee that the procedures for protecting Community funds are complied with, whatever the entity responsible for all or part of this implementation and must confirm that final responsibility for budgetary implementation lies with the Commission in accordance with Art. 274 of the Treaty" (see Financial Regulation (EC) No. 1605/2002 of 13 December 2006, op. cit., Recital No. 16). The Commission's full responsibility is reiterated in Recital No. 37. Several judgements of the European Court of Justice have confirmed this interpretation (see for example, Case law C-16/88, *Commission v. Council* [1989] ECR I-3457, para. 15; Case law C-106/96, *UK v. Commission* [1998] ECR I-2729, para. 15).

[281] See Box 5.1.

[282] See European Court of Auditors, Opinion No. 6/2007 of 19 June 2007 on the annual summaries of member states, 'national declarations' of member states and audit work on EU funds of national audit bodies, Luxembourg, para. XI.

[283] The new reform Treaty for Europe, agreed by EU heads of state and government in Lisbon (18-19 October 2007), will modify article 274 of the EC treaty along the lines of the modifications agreed in article III-407 of the Treaty establishing a Constitution for Europe. In particular, the new provision emphasises that the budget is implemented by the Commission "in cooperation with the Member

Concerning in particular the issue of sound financial management, one should note that practically all efforts in the reform of the EU's financial management have been concentrated on the conformity of EU budget expenditure with specific eligibility conditions. Most of the rules were and are devised primarily with the objective of ensuring compliance in terms of the legality of expenditure. The European Parliament has indeed pointed out that "the focus actually given to the legality and regularity of the spending does not help to inform the legislator and the public as to whether the money has been spent effectively".[284] Moreover, the 'regularity' of expenditure does not ensure that the objectives have been met, which are, for example in the case of structural policies, "reducing disparities between the levels of development of the various regions".[285] Indeed, it has been observed that "there can be projects, brilliantly executed in terms of formal rules and formulas, but still failing in achieving any objective, and vice versa".[286]

In this respect, one should note that there seems to be an unclear understanding of the concept of sound financial management. For example, the Interinstitutional Agreement for the 2007–13 financial framework provides that "priority will be given to sound financial management aiming at a positive Statement of Assurance, for funds under shared management", however referring back to the assessment concerning the compliance of management and control systems with the regulations of the Community to be produced by the member states.[287] Similarly, the director-generals at the Commission have confirmed that they have obtained reasonable assurance that the resources allocated to the activities of their directorate-general have been used "for their intended purpose and in

---

States" and that "the control and audit obligations of the Member States in the implementation of the budget and the resulting responsibilities" will be fixed by regulation.

[284] See European Parliament, Resolution of 12 April 2005 (op. cit.), para. 32(d).

[285] See Art. 158 TEC.

[286] See the speech of Siim Kallas of 23 October 2006 before the European Parliament Budgetary Control Committee (Kallas, 2006).

[287] See European Parliament, Council and Commission (2006), para. 44.

accordance with the principles of sound financial management".[288] On what ground this assurance is based, remains vague. The parameter under consideration is the legality of spending: an audit of the performance of projects is not a current practice at the Commission.

Actually, the concept of value for money is now well defined by the Financial Regulation. The Regulation provides that the appropriations shall be used "in accordance with the principles of economy, efficiency and effectiveness", that "specific, measurable, achievable, relevant and timed objectives shall be set for all sectors of activity covered by the budget", that "achievement of those objectives shall be monitored by performance indicators for each activity" and also that "information shall be provided by the spending authorities to the budgetary authority". The Regulation finally provides that the institutions "shall undertake both ex ante and ex post evaluations in line with guidance provided by the Commission. Such evaluations shall be applied to all programmes and activities which entail significant spending and evaluation results disseminated to spending, legislative and budgetary authorities."[289] Yet, concerning the evaluations,

---

[288] See for example the following European Commission reports: *Annual Activity Report for the Year 2006*, DG Regional Policy, Brussels, 30 March 2007(f), (p. 47); *2006 Annual Activity Report*, DG Employment, Social Affairs and Equal Opportunity, Brussels, 28 March 2007(g), (p. 54); and *Annual Activity Report 2006*, DG Fisheries and Maritime Affairs, Brussels, 29 March 2007(h), (p. 41).

[289] See Art. 27 of Council Regulation (EC, Euratom) No. 1605/2002 of 13 December 2006 (op. cit.). The concept of 'sound financial management' made a late appearance in the provisions of the Treaty concerning the implementation of the budget. True, as early as in the Treaty establishing the European Economic Community (1957), auditing the budget had been entrusted to an Audit Board with the purpose of establishing that "the financial management has been sound" (Art. 206 TEC). But sound financial management is one of the principles applied to EU spending only since 1990, when the Financial Regulation was modified (Council Regulation (Euratom, ECSC, EEC) No. 610/90 of 13 March 1990 amending the Financial Regulation of 21 December 1977 applicable to the general budget of the European Communities, OJ L 70, 16.3.1990) to provide that "the budget appropriations must be used in accordance with the principles of sound financial management, and in particular those of economy and cost-effectiveness. Quantified objectives must be identified and the progress of their realization monitored." The concept was subsequently enshrined in the Maastricht Treaty on European Union in 1992 where a few words were added to Art. 205 (nowadays

the specific rules applicable to the structural policies[290] constitute an exception to the general principles of the Financial Regulation. First, the Commission's guidance on evaluation methods, including quality standards, must be agreed upon with the member states and it will remain indicative. Also, contrary to the provisions of the Financial Regulation, *ex ante* evaluations are carried out by the member states. The Commission may carry out strategic evaluations and, in partnership with the member state concerned, evaluations linked to the monitoring of operational programmes where the monitoring of programmes reveals a significant departure from the goals initially set. The Commission is nevertheless responsible for *ex post* evaluations. The economy, efficiency and effectiveness of expenditures are issues that are essentially dealt with later at the EU level in the evaluation process, with the limitations therein.[291]

Concluding remarks

It seems clear that shared management arrangements result in weaker accountability. This 'cost' is in the end a political choice. In addition, the increased emphasis on the compliance of EU budget expenditure with specific eligibility conditions has made the concept of value for money a kind of 'poor relation' in this context. The process of progressively discharging its management responsibilities to third parties (for example

---

Art. 274) of the EC Treaty, to indicate that the budget is implemented "in accordance with the principles of sound financial management". In 1995, the Financial Regulation was modified again (Council Regulation (EC, Euratom, ECSC) No. 2333/95 of 18 September 1995, amending the Financial Regulation of 21 December 1977 applicable to the general budget of the European Communities, OJ L 240, 7.10.1995), providing that the "mobilization of Community resources must be preceded by an evaluation to ensure that the resultant benefits are in proportion to the resources applied. All operations must be subject to regular review, in particular within the budgetary procedure, so that their justification may be verified." The present provisions on sound financial management were introduced by the Financial Regulation recasting of 2002.

[290] See Council Regulation (EC) No. 1083/2006 of 11 November 2006 (op. cit.), especially Arts 47 to 49. See also European Commission, *Indicative Guidelines on Evaluation Methods: Evaluation during the programming period*, Working Document No. 5, April 2007(m).

[291] See European Court of Auditors (2006a) and European Parliament (2006).

the member states and executive agencies) gives rise to the question of whether the Commission is not actually retracing its steps, gradually becoming once again an institution that devises and proposes policies instead of one that implements programmes.

All responsible, nobody responsible?

Experience suggests that separating responsibility from management has led to a shuttling of responsibilities backwards and forwards between the Commission and member states, agencies and other delegated bodies. In these circumstances, it is often difficult to identify who should do what to remedy a problem. As has been observed,

> The member states have a conflict of interest. On the one hand as members of the Council it is their duty in adopting regulations to create conditions for their implementation that are readily implemented and controlled by the Commission. On the other hand as nation states they favour their own systems of management and control. This hybrid arrangement leads to a lack of clarity on mutual responsibilities and obligations and fails to give any guarantee that the right balance has been struck in the interests of good management of Community monies.[292]

The *millefeuille* of procedures, intervention levels and management and control bodies that characterises budgetary implementation in shared management arrangements inevitably brings with it the dilution of the responsibilities of the various protagonists. In the absence of a 'taker' for genuine final responsibility, the budgetary implementation is subject de facto to a limited form of responsibility. One can even wonder whether the defining characteristic of budgetary implementation under shared management is not in fact the absence of full control by the Commission. Because if the Commission did have full control, it would end up in conflict with the prerogatives of the member states, thus upsetting the institutional balance laid down by the Treaty. It is clear, however, that if the full

---

[292] See Committee of Independent Experts (1999b), para. 3.5.3. It is worth noting that the Financial Regulation establishes the principle that "all financial actors and any other person involved in budget implementation, management, audit or control shall be prohibited from taking any action which may bring their own interests into conflict with those of the Communities" (see Art. 52(1) of Council Regulation (EC, Euratom) No. 1605/2002 of 13 December 2006, op. cit.).

responsibility borne by the Commission were to disappear, the measures that are the subject of shared management would inevitably be subject to nothing more than self-audit by the member states themselves. This approach would put the member states in a situation that would have all the characteristics of a 'potestative' state.[293]

It is by means of the discharge procedure that "the right to ask a public official for an accounting of his administration" is materialised.[294] Indeed, the discharge procedure constitutes not only the formal act of closing the accounts, but also represents an opportunity for a political judgment on the way the Commission has discharged its responsibilities.[295]

Yet, in the field of shared or decentralised management, the exercise of presenting the accounts concerning the funds spent through the Community budget has traditionally proved to be extremely difficult. The separation of responsibilities as regards implementation objectively deprives the European Parliament of a real interlocutor. In this respect, the European Court of Auditors has expressed concern that "if the Commission no longer had final responsibility for implementing the budget, the Community's financial process, and in particular the discharge procedure, would lose a good deal of its significance. The budgetary authorities' recommendations (Art. 276 (3) of the EC Treaty) would be deprived of all practical effect."[296]

---

[293] In its conclusions concerning Case C-16/88, *Commission v. Council* [1989] ECR, p. 3480, the Court of Justice of 24 October 1989, Advocate General Darmon envisaged the possibility of a 'potestative' situation where the Council "would ultimately have the power to empty of their substance the powers" of the Commission.

[294] See Art. 15 of the Declaration of the Rights of Man and the Citizen (National Assembly of France, 26 August 1789). The glossary of terms of the European Court of Auditors gives this definition: "Accountability means the obligations of persons or entities, including public enterprises and corporations, entrusted with public resources to be answerable for the fiscal, managerial and programme responsibilities that have been conferred on them, and to report to those that have conferred these responsibilities on them."

[295] For example, Art. 201 TEC envisages the resignation of the Commission as a result of the passing of a motion of censure by the European Parliament.

[296] See European Court of Auditors, Opinion No. 2/2005 of 18 March 2005 (op. cit.), para. 6.

The Commission does not hesitate to point out the responsibilities specifically allocated to the member states whenever management on the ground is challenged. As a matter of example, the Court recently noted for an operational programme on structural policies that despite an initial intention to spend approximately equal amounts on road and rail, "on absorption grounds it was proposed to allocate all of the performance reserve to road construction", so not "in line with environmental or transport policy objectives, but according to progress in spending". The Commission replied that it was not 'happy' with this high allocation of funding to the transport infrastructure, especially the road infrastructure. It claimed nonetheless that it has regularly raised the matter with the member state concerned and will "take up this point in the negotiations for the next programme period".[297] Again, to a Court report observing that "despite problems in the set-up and management of the ERF [European refugee fund], there were numerous positive examples of management systems", the Commission replied that these examples demonstrate that the legal provisions and guidance provided by the Commission have helped the member states "which wished to do so" to build sound control systems.[298]

Meanwhile, the European Parliament does not have the authority to question national administrations regarding their management of Community funds. In such a situation, the share of the budgetary implementation that has been 'devolved' to the member states – more than 80% it must be pointed out – is likely ultimately to escape any genuine exercise of the rendering of accounts.

Concluding remarks

The identification of clear and complete responsibility regarding the implementation of the Community budget might well condition its development as much as the volume of the appropriations to be authorised, the level of the contributions to be paid by each member state and the typology of the policies to be financed. There is in fact no valid reason the

---

[297] See European Court of Auditors, *Special Report No. 1/2007 concerning the implementation of the mid-term processes on the Structural Funds 2000–06*, OJ C 124, 5.6.2007(a), para. 33.

[298] See European Court of Auditors, *Special Report No. 3/2007 concerning the management of the European Refugee Fund*, Luxembourg, OJ C 178, 31.7.2007(b), para. 37.

implementation of the Community budget, which is financed by the European taxpayer through general taxation, should not be subject to the principle of responsibility, one of the fundamental principles of public finance.

6. THREE UNAVOIDABLE REFORMS

The price 'paid' (or maybe one of its achievements) for the necessarily unanimous agreement on the 2007–13 financial perspective was the European Council's decision "that the EU should carry out a comprehensive reassessment of the financial framework, covering both revenue and expenditure, to sustain modernisation and to enhance it, on an ongoing basis".[299] The idea of a review of the EU budget is actually not new.[300] The fact is, however, that past reviews have not succeeded in

---

[299] See European Council (2005a), para. 79. The document states that the agreement consists of three parts (expenditure, revenue and review) considered "complementary and inseparable". The intention was that all aspects of the EU budget would be examined in 2008–09, and that this process could lead to fundamental reform. In particular, the UK government made a clear and categorical link between the UK rebate and the fundamental reform of expenditure across the EU, notably the issue of the CAP.

[300] The 1988 Own Resources Decision had already required the Commission to "submit, by the end of 1991, a report on the operation of the system, including a re-examination of the correction of budgetary imbalances granted to the United Kingdom" (see Council Decision 88/376/EEC, Euratom of 24 June 1988, op. cit., Art. 10). The same request was repeated by the 1994 Own Resources Decision, with the Commission also asked to submit, by the end of 1999, "a report on the findings of a study on the feasibility of creating a new own resource, as well as on arrangements for the possible introduction of a fixed uniform rate applicable to the VAT base" (see Council Decision 94/728/EC, Euratom of 31 October 1994, op. cit., Art. 10). Finally, the 2000 Own Resources Decision asked the Commission to

> undertake, before 1 January 2006, a general review of the own resources system, accompanied, if necessary, by appropriate proposals, in the light of all relevant factors, including the effects of enlargement on the financing of the budget, the possibility of modifying the structure of the own resources by creating new autonomous own resources and the correction of budgetary imbalances granted to the UK as well as the granting to Austria, Germany,

solving these problems or even in bringing some progress. On the contrary, each review has increased the lack of transparency and found short-sighted solutions, entirely subservient to the achievement of a unanimous agreement among member states. The EU's finances have developed in fits and starts, according to the expediency of the most urgent 'needs' taking precedence over a consistent budgetary design for key features, such as revenue, expenditure and, not least, accountability.

One might form the impression that, in the end, it is all a question of money. Yet this conclusion seems reductive, as the defence of purely national financial interests often reveals only the first layer of a wider reality. Behind the scenes, sensitive matters such the unanimity rule, the institutional balance of powers between the European institutions (for example, in deciding the amount, type and management of the EU's budget revenue and expenditure) and the role of national parliaments are at stake.

The weaknesses of the EU financial framework are not attributable to a supposedly wrong conceptual design, but rather derive from the EU integration process. This is why it would not seem appropriate to restrict the incoming reform review to an academic debate. If there is one subject that has been thoroughly explored for many years it is the EU's finances. Institutional actors, such as the Commission[301] or the European Parliament[302] and many academic experts[303] have all provided valuable and largely converging diagnoses and each put forward their own 'therapy'. The time seems therefore ripe not for a study but for a decision process about possible solutions. The incoming review is at once an opportunity and a difficult challenge, unpredictable in its outcome. As such, the EU budget is a key condition for the evolution of European integration and

---

the Netherlands and Sweden of the reduction. (Council Decision 2000/597/EC, Euratom of 29 September 2000, op. cit., Art. 9)

[301] See the European Commission reports on the own resources (European Commission, 1998, and Vol. I and Vol. II, 2004f and 2004g).

[302] See the European Parliament reports (1994a and 1994b). See also the report by the European Parliament, *Report on Policy Challenges and Budgetary Means of the Enlarged Union 2007–2013*, Temporary Committee on Policy Challenges and Budgetary Means of the enlarged Union 2007-2013, Rapporteur: R. Böge, A6-0153/2005, 19 May 2005(b).

[303] See, for example, footnote 4.

part of the debate on the legitimacy of the Union's actions. It cannot remain an issue among governments alone.[304] Indeed, to debate the EU budget is actually to discuss visions of Europe's future, starting from the role of EU institutions.

The coming reform will have to deal with fundamental issues, such as the volume of the EU budget and by what kind of revenue it should be financed; if and to what extent the EU budget should finance redistributive, allocative or stabilising policies; whether some policies should be discontinued and, in particular, whether the EU budget should continue to finance agricultural spending;[305] whether a larger share of the EU budget should be reserved for research spending; and whether structural policies should be re-directed towards a limited number of regions.

These are key political issues that are not examined as such in the present study. It seems nonetheless that the inconsistencies and problems that have been described in the previous sections can be reduced to a large extent to a common denominator: the lack of a link with the taxpayers, the lack of a proper intervention logic and a delivery deficit about the results

---

[304] In this respect, it is to be welcomed that the Commission launched a broad consultation to stimulate an open debate on the EU's finances (see European Commission, "Reforming the Budget, Changing Europe: A Public Consultation Paper in View of the 2008/2009 Budget Review", Brussels, September 2007(s)).

[305] The general public does not seem to share the rather negative opinion of academic experts about the financing of the CAP through the EU budget. A survey carried out at the end of 2006 shows that, in response to the question of whether the current agriculture and rural development budget is "insufficient, adequate or too high" (knowing that CAP financing represents "around 40%" of the whole EU budget), a large section of the public endorses the current level of agricultural expenditure. The majority (45%) thinks that the current proportion of the budget devoted to agriculture is "about right". This share outnumbers the combined figure for those who think that the budget is "insufficient" (15%) or "too high" (16%). In the UK, despite a reputation for being anti-farm spending, 40% of those polled said that the EU's current farm budget was suitable (11% said it was not high enough and 20% said it was too high). When it comes to the question of the CAP budget in the future, the picture is slightly less clear. Nevertheless, the dominating view held by over half (58%) is that the share of the total EU budget taken up by agriculture should at the very least stay the same, if not increase (see European Commission, *Europeans, Agricultural and the Common Agricultural Policy*, Special Eurobarometer No. 276, Brussels, March 2007(i)).

achieved. In this respect there are three issues, inextricably interlinked, on which the common interest of all concerned (above all the member states) should be found, thus ensuring that the coming review does not become a losing battle. These issues are revenue, results and responsibility.

Revenue: One system for all

There are numerous possibilities for a new system of revenue for the EU budget. These go from the very 'simple' solution of a contribution scale by member state,[306] through a classical system of financing based on a GNI allocation key, to tax-based resources such as a genuine VAT resource. A mix of different types of resources is also imaginable. Within this framework, an almost infinite number of suboptions could be envisaged, each having different political implications (above all the issue of fiscal sovereignty) and a variable financial weight for the member states. One might wonder, however, whether agreement could not be reached on three elements:

- Whatever the system, it should be applicable to all member states in the same way.[307] Also, it should be a built-to-last system, not subject to change at each financial perspective with a view to accommodating specific claims. Exceptions should not be a subject of negotiation.

- Any imbalances should be examined in the context of the expenditure side, by assessing the economic impact of the policies on the various economies. From this point of view, there would be no place for budgetary balances and special revenue arrangements. This approach would, in a way, simply recognise what the Council decided in 1999 – a system that should be "equitable, transparent, cost-effective and

---

[306] In the founding EEC Treaty, the financing of the budget was based on a percentage share by member state, although differently concerning the European social fund expenditure (see footnote 102). For a review of the different options examined, see the European Commission reports on the own resources (European Commission, 1998 and Vol. I, 2004f).

[307] For example, the European Parliament has stressed "that any new system of own resources – regardless of its structure – must be applicable to all member states in accordance with the same principle". See European Parliament, Resolution of 11 March 2003 on reform of the budgetary procedure: Possible options in view of the revision of the Treaties, para. 17.

simple", resolving possible budgetary imbalances "by means of expenditure policy".[308]

- The volume of the EU budget is such that it is no longer possible to avoid raising European citizens' awareness of the cost of European-driven policies. It is only if this link is made that one can expect more commitment from them, and consequently greater accountability, presently rather weak, on the part of the policy actors. As has been observed, "Citizens of each member state elect their Government on the basis of their proposed distribution of resources and level of public spending, and on the types and level of taxation required to deliver these. This is fundamental to the democratic control and accountability of government and results in a greater acceptance of taxation decisions by individual electorates."[309] The best way of achieving this would be to introduce a genuine European tax, preferably a VAT resource that would fulfil all the guiding criteria, including the advantage of being an existing tax.

Still, if the time has not yet come for such a tax and a system of national contributions is maintained, this should not be detrimental to the need for better awareness about what is disbursed and for the benefit of whom. There is no reason, when national finance laws are the subject of (sometimes huge) debates, for the same not to happen at the European level. Indeed, in one way or another, citizens should be made aware of the 'cost of Europe'. Without transparency, the low level of confidence among public opinion about the way the EU spends its money can only fall even further.

Results: Fewer, better targeted and verifiable objectives

We must put member states and institutions on their guard against overlarge or ill-defined projects, in whatever area of policy these may be proposed, which would be ill-suited to the Community's present stage of development and would consume quantities of money and effort without appreciable results. Such projects must be defensible

---

[308] See European Council (1999), points 65–66.

[309] See European Convention, Contribution to the European Convention, Articles III.59 and III.60 in the draft EU Constitutional Treaty (submitted by P. Hain et al.), CONV 782/03, Brussels, 3 June 2003(e).

on their own merits and certainly should not be advocated as a means of correcting budgetary imbalances in the Community.[310]

This rather old warning still seems relevant today. The question here is two-fold: Can there really be European added value almost everywhere? And is there a risk that the EU budget may fund so many policies that, in the end, this will result in limited impact given the restriction on the financial resources available? In the end, one cannot have one's cake and eat it. The traffic jam produced by a multiplicity of objectives and actions is detrimental in many respects. The size of the policies, if they are to have a clear and visible impact, matters much more than the size of the budget itself. Lack of proven effectiveness does not enhance the merits of EU actions; nor does it strengthen the much-needed accountability. In the end, the limited size of the EU budget should be taken as an advantage and could be used as an argument for selectivity. It would be unwise to "saddle the Union with a set of goals and then deny it the resources required".[311] Indeed, EU spending "must be organised in such a way that the spending meets its goals. Optimising EU spending is therefore about choices, and about concentrating resources where they generate the highest profit." [312]

There are also in this context three elements on which agreement should be reached as a precondition for progress:

- Discussions of a future financial perspective should not start with the overall amount of resources put at the disposal of the EU budget. It seems more reasonable that the process should rather start with an examination of the proposed policies, on the basis of their own merits, but also of their costs, including 'delivery' costs such as the administrative costs of designing, implementing, monitoring and *ex post* evaluating any given policy.

- When selecting a policy and deciding upon a programme, the institutional actors should also fix the objectives to be achieved by the beneficiaries and make sure that these will be verifiable in practice. In this respect, making full use of the funds cannot be in itself an objective. The legality of spending should not override considerations about value for money.

---

[310] See the 'Report of the Three Wise Men' by Biesheuvel, Dell & Marjolin (1979).

[311] See European Commission (2004a), p. 26.

[312] See European Commission (2007s), p. 7.

- There are probably good reasons for fixing a multi-annual financial framework, above all the need for a certain stability. Yet one should question whether the current practice of committing the whole appropriations at the beginning of the financial perspective (in particular for structural policies) should not be relaxed. This change would make it possible to take account of new emerging priorities and take corrective action during the execution of programmes. Not least, this would make the annual budgetary procedure more meaningful.

Responsibility: A single, fully endorsed, responsibility

The Commission has rightly said that "[t]axpayers should have reasonable assurance that the funds of the European Union are managed in a legal and regular manner".[313] This assurance is all the more necessary as the absence of a direct link between European taxpayers and the Community budget encourages the false idea that these funds grow on trees and that they therefore constitute a kind of 'manna'. Full responsibility and good management are closely interlinked. The implementation of the EU budget must give the taxpayer (and the potential recipients of its policies) the same guarantees that exist in respect of national budgets.

Logic would plead in favour of a single, undivided responsibility. This question is one of political priorities. If shared management is to remain the main type of management system, it is inevitable that full accountability will not be achieved. If in practice the bulk of the expenditure is devolved to the member states (the design of actions, implementation and control), it should not be surprising to observe that the effectiveness of this expenditure will actually be proportional to the trouble the member states take to ensure value for money. Despite all the Commission's efforts, in the end the member states will take the key decisions.

Concerning the issue of responsibility, there are also three elements where, if not agreement, at least awareness could be reached:

- It would be difficult to achieve full accountability in the case of shared management, especially in a system where a limited number of sanctions exist and where these very often do not target the

---

[313] See European Commission (2005h), p. 2.

beneficiaries, but rather constitute further expenditure charged to the national budgets. This situation could be changed, by making the faulty beneficiaries directly and financially answerable.

- Without full accountability, the discharge procedure for the EU budget, which is exclusively directed towards the Commission, will probably become less and less significant and needs to be seriously rethought. As it would not be imaginable to summon 27 member states (or their administrations) before the European Parliament, the question is whether, having delegated the management of a significant part of the budget to member states, the discharge procedure should not also involve increasingly national Parliaments. The recent move towards the establishment of national declarations on the use of EU funds in certain member states seems to point in that direction.

- Finally yet importantly, is accountability to the European citizens. They contribute to the EU budget but, even more crucially, they expect that whoever is made responsible in the end will be easily identifiable. An acceptable solution to the issue of responsibility in executing the EU budget would also contribute to the legitimacy of the EU's actions. As the European Council recently concluded, "[W]e have to maintain and develop the European Union's capacity to act and its accountability to the citizen".[314]

---

[314] See European Council, Presidency Conclusions of the Brussels European Council of 21-22 June, 11177/1/07 REV 1, Brussels, 20 July 2007(b), point 2.

BIBLIOGRAPHY

Alesina, A., I. Angeloni and L. Schuknecht (2002), *What Does the European Union Do?*, RSC No. 2002/61, Robert Schuman Centre for Advanced Studies, European University Institute, Florence.

Amato, G. and M. Marè (2005), "Using a New VAT for Taxing Consumption and Financing the EU Budget", mimeo, Rome, August.

Baldwin, R. (2005), *The Real Budget Battle*, Policy Brief No. 75, CEPS, Brussels, June.

Begg, I. (2004), *The EU budget: Common future or stuck in the past?*, Centre for European Reform, London, February.

————— (2005), *Funding the European Union: Making Sense of the EU Budget*, A Federal Trust Report on the European Union's Budget, Federal Trust for Education and Research, London, March.

Begg, I., N. Grimwade and P. Price (1997), *Les ressources propres de l'Union européenne: analyse et développements possibles*, Working Document, European Parliament, September.

Begg, I. and F. Heinemann (2006), *New budget, old dilemmas*, Centre for European Reform, London, February.

Berglof, E., B. Eichengreen, G. Roland, G. Tabellini and C. Wyplosz (2002), *Built to Last: A Political Architecture for Europe*, Centre for Economic and Policy Research, London.

Biesheuvel, B., E. Dell and F.R. Marjolin (1979), *Report on the European Institutions* ('Report of the Three Wise Men'), Presented by the Committee of Three to the European Council, Office for Official Publications of the European Communities, Luxembourg, October.

Blankart, C. and C. Kirchner (2003), *The deadlock of the EU budget: An economic analysis of ways in and ways out*, Working Paper No. 989, CESifo, Munich.

Buti, M. and M. Nava (2003), *Towards a European Budgetary System*, RSC No. 2003/08, Robert Schuman Centre for Advanced Studies, European University Institute, Florence.

Castagnède, B. (2002), « Souveraineté fiscale et Union européenne », *Revue Française de Finances Publiques*, No. 80, December.

Cattoir, P. (2004), *Tax-based EU own resources: An assessment*, Working Paper No. 1/2004, DG for Taxation and Customs Union, European Commission, Brussels, April.

Cipriani, G. (2006), *The Responsibility for Implementing the Community Budget*, CEPS Working Document No. 247, CEPS, Brussels, June.

Cipriani, G. and M. Marè (2003), *La finanza dell'Unione europea tra allargamento e ambizioni federali*, Consiglio Nazionale dell'Economia e del Lavoro, Rome, July.

Cipriani, G. and C. Polito (2003), *Le statistiche di contabilità nazionale: un controllo dei dati è possibile ?*, Working Paper No. 195, Società italiana di economia pubblica, Pavia, January.

Cipriani, G. and S. Pisani (2004), *The European budget: An alternative to budgetary balances to assess benefits for the member states*, Working Paper No. 339, Società italiana di economia pubblica, Pavia, October.

Committee of Independent Experts (1999a), *First Report on Allegations Regarding Fraud, Mismanagement and Nepotism in the European Commission*, Brussels, 15 March.

————— (1999b), *Second Report on Reform of the Commission: Analysis of current practice and proposals for tackling mismanagement, irregularities and fraud*, Brussels, 10 September.

De la Fuente, A. and R. Domenéch (2000), "The redistributive effects of the EU budget: An analysis and a proposal for reform", mimeo, February.

Denton, G. (1984), "Re-structuring the EC Budget: Implications of the Fontainebleau Agreement", *Journal of Common Market Studies*, Vol. XXIII, No. 2, December.

Economic and Financial Affairs Committee (Ecofin) (2003), Council Conclusions, 5936/03, Brussels, 18 February.

————— (2004a), Council Conclusions, 14429/04, Brussels, 16 November.

————— (2004b), Council Conclusions, 9779/04, Brussels, 2 June.

————— (2005), Council Conclusions, 13678/05, Brussels, 8 November.

Ederveen, S., J. Gorter and R. Nahuis (2001), "The Wealth of Regions: The Impact of Structural Funds on Convergence in the EU", mimeo, Netherlands Bureau for Economic Policy Analysis, The Hague.

Ehlermann, C.D. (1982), "The Financing of the Community: The distinction between financial contributions and own resources", *Common Market Law Review*, Vol. 19, No. 4.

Enderlein, H., J. Lindner, O. Calvo-Gonzalez and R. Ritter (2005), *The EU Budget: How much scope for institutional reform?*, Occasional Paper No. 27, European Central Bank, Frankfurt, April.

European Commission (1965), « Financement de la politique agricole commune - Ressources propres de la Communauté – Renforcement des pouvoirs du Parlement européen », COM(65) 150, Brussels, 31 March.

————— (1974), "Inventory of the Community's economic and financial situation since enlargement and survey of future developments", *Supplement to the Bulletin 7/74*, Brussels, 27 October.

————— (1977), *Report by the Study Group on the Role of Public Finance in European Integration*, Rapporteurs: D. MacDougal et al., Luxembourg, April.

————— (1978), *Global appraisal of the budgetary problems of the Community*, COM(78) 64, Brussels, 27 February.

————— (1979), *Reference paper on budgetary questions*, COM(79) 462, Brussels, 12 September.

————— (1980), Communication on Convergence and Budgetary Questions, COM(80) 147, Brussels, 20 March.

————— (1981), *Report on the Application of the Financial Mechanism*, COM(81) 704 final, Brussels, 13 November.

————— (1987), *Report by the Commission to the Council and Parliament on the Financing of the Community Budget*, COM(87) 101, Brussels, 28 February.

————— (1997a), *Agenda 2000, Communication for a Stronger and Wider Union*, Vol. I, 97/6, Brussels, 15 July.

————— (1997b), *Budget Contributions, EU Expenditure, Budgetary Balances and Relative Prosperity of the Member States*, Paper presented by President Jacques Santer to the Ecofin Council, Brussels, 13 October.

————— (1998), *Financing the European Union, Commission report on the operation of the own resources system*, COM(1998) 560, Brussels, 7 October.

———— (2000), White Paper on Reforming the Commission, COM(2000) 200, Brussels, 1 March.

———— (2001), Communication on adaptation of the ceiling of own resources and of the ceiling for appropriations for commitments following the entry into force of Decision 2000/597/EC, Euratom, COM(2001) 801, Brussels, 28 December.

———— (2002a), *European Union Public Finance*, Luxembourg.

———— (2002b), *Report Concerning the Allocation of Financial Intermediation Services Indirectly Measured (FISIM) containing a qualitative and quantitative analysis of the results of the trial calculations for allocating and calculating FISIM as described in the Council Regulation (EC) No. 448/98 of 16 February 1998*, COM(2002) 333/F, Brussels, 21 June.

———— (2002c), Communication on the need and the means to upgrade the quality of budgetary statistics, COM(2002) 670, Brussels, 11 November.

———— (2002d), Communication on a Project for the European Union, COM(2002) 247 final, Brussels, 22 May.

———— (2003a), "EU fundamentally reforms its farm policy to accomplish sustainable farming in Europe", Press release, IP/03/898, Brussels, 26 June.

———— (2003b), *Updated check-list of administrative conditions in the area of the European Communities' own resources*, Brussels, November.

———— (2004a), *Building our common future: Policy challenges and budgetary means of the enlarged Union 2007–13*, COM(2004) 101, Brussels, 26 February.

———— (2004b), Communication on the Financial Perspective 2007–13, COM(2004) 487, Brussels, 14 July.

———— (2004c), *Proposal of a legislative package revising the regulations applicable to the management of the Structural and of Cohesion Funds: Analysis of impact in the enlarged Union*, Commission Working Paper, SEC(2004) 924, Brussels, 14 July.

———— (2004d), *Five-Year Assessment of the European Union Research Framework Programmes 1999–2003*, Brussels, December.

———— (2004e), *Evaluating EU activities – A Practical Guide for Commission Services*, Brussels, July.

——————— (2004f), *Financing the European Union, Commission report on the operation of the own resources system*, Vol. I, COM(2004) 505 final, Brussels, 14 July.

——————— (2004g), *Technical Annex, Financing the European Union, Commission report on the operation of the own resources system*, Vol. II, COM(2004) 505 final, Brussels, 14 July.

——————— (2004h), "Statement by Commissioner Joaquín Almunia on the revision of Greek deficit and debt data", Press release, IP/04/1135, Brussels, 23 September.

——————— (2004i), *Report on the Accountability Issue related to the Revision of Greek Budgetary Data*, COM(2004) 784, Brussels, 1 December.

——————— (2004j), Communication, Towards a European Governance Strategy for Fiscal Statistics, COM(2004) 832, Brussels, 22 December.

——————— (2004k), *Proposal for a Council Decision on the system of the European Communities' own resources*, COM(2004) 501, Brussels, 3 August.

——————— (2004l), *Proposal for a Council Regulation laying down general provisions on the European Regional Development Fund, the European Social Fund and the Cohesion Fund*, COM(2004) 492, Brussels, 14 July.

——————— (2004m), Communication on a Synthesis of 2003 Annual Activity Reports of DGs and Services, COM(2004) 418 final, Brussels, 19 July.

——————— (2005a), "Five proposals to relaunch negotiations", Memo/05/386, Brussels, 20 October.

——————— (2005b), *Impact assessment and* ex ante *evaluation of the 7th Framework Programme*, Main Report and Annex 1, SEC(2005) 430, Brussels, 6 April.

——————— (2005c), "Why Europe Needs Research Spending", Memo/05/199, Brussels, 9 June.

——————— (2005d), *Replacing the VAT resource by the GNI-based own resource*, Working Document, Multi-annual Financial Framework 2007-2013, Fiche No. 85, Brussels, 18 February.

——————— (2005e), Communication on the Independence, Accountability and Integrity of the National and Community Statistical Authorities, COM(2005) 217 final, Brussels, 25 May.

———— (2005f), "Calculating member states' net budgetary balances", Document prepared for the European Council's Working Group on Own Resources, Brussels, 21 February.

———— (2005g), Communication on a Progress report on the Commission reform beyond the reform mandate, COM(2005) 668, Brussels, 21 December.

———— (2005h), Communication on a roadmap to an integrated internal control framework, COM(2005) 252, Brussels, 15 June.

———— (2005i), *A gap assessment between the internal control framework in the Commission Services, and the control principles set out in the Court of Auditors' "proposal for a Community internal control framework" Opinion No. 2/2004*, Commission Staff Working Document, SEC(2005) 1152, Brussels, 28 September.

———— (2005j), *Report from the Commission on Member States' replies to the Court of Auditors' 2002 Annual Report*, COM(2004) 859, Brussels, 5 January.

———— (2005k), Communication from the President in agreement with Vice-President Wallström, Strategic Objectives 2005–2009, Europe 2010: A Partnership for European Renewal, Prosperity, Solidarity and Security, COM(2005) 12 final, Brussels, 26 January.

———— (2006a), Communication on Implementing the Renewed Lisbon Strategy for Growth and Jobs: "A year of delivery", COM(2006) 816, Brussels, 12 December.

———— (2006b), Communication on Enlargement Strategy and Main Challenges 2006–07, COM(2006) 649, Brussels, 8 November.

———— (2006c), *Evaluation of the EU programme to promote member state co-operation to combat social exclusion and poverty*, Main Report, December.

———— (2006d), Communication on the Growth and Jobs Strategy and the Reform of European cohesion policy: Fourth progress report on cohesion, COM(2006) 281 final, Brussels, 12 December.

———— (2006e), Communication on Policy Achievements in 2005, COM(2006) 124, Brussels, 14 March.

———— (2006f), *Structures of the taxation systems in the European Union: 1995–2004*, Doc. Taxud e4/2006/doc/3201, Brussels.

————— (2006g), "Lisbon Strategy for Growth and Jobs: Frequently asked questions", Memo 06/474, Brussels, 8 December.

————— (2006h), Communication on a Commission Action Plan towards an Integrated Internal Control Framework, COM(2006) 9, Brussels, 17 January.

————— (2006i), *Report on budgetary and financial management accompanying the Community accounts, Financial Year 2006*, DG Budget, Brussels.

————— (2006j), "Q&A on Interinstitutional Agreement on Budgetary Discipline and Sound Financial Management 2007-2013", Memo/06/204, Brussels, 17 May.

————— (2007a), "Low business R&D a major threat to European knowledge-based economy", Press release, IP/07/790, Brussels, 11 June.

————— (2007b), *Key Figures 2007 on Science, Technology and Innovation: Towards a European Knowledge Area*, Brussels, 11 June.

————— (2007c), Communication on Policy Achievements in 2006, COM(2007) 67, Brussels, 28 February.

————— (2007d), Communication on the Synthesis of the Commission's Management Achievements in 2006, COM(2007) 274, Brussels, 30 May.

————— (2007e), Communication on the Annual Evaluation Review 2006, COM(2007) 300, Brussels, May.

————— (2007f), *Annual Activity Report for the Year 2006*, DG Regional Policy, Brussels, 30 March.

————— (2007g), *2006 Annual Activity Report*, DG Employment, Social Affairs and Equal Opportunity, Brussels, 28 March.

————— (2007h), *Annual Activity Report 2006*, DG Fisheries and Maritime Affairs, Brussels, 29 March.

————— (2007i), *Europeans, Agricultural and the Common Agricultural Policy*, Special Eurobarometer No. 276, Brussels, March.

————— (2007j), Financial Programming 2007–13, DG Budget, Brussels, 26 January.

————— (2007k), Communication on Galileo at a cross-road: The implementation of the European GNSS programmes, COM(2007) 261 final, Brussels, May.

——————— (2007l), *EU Budget 2006 – Financial Report*, Brussels, September.

——————— (2007m), *Indicative Guidelines on Evaluation Methods: Evaluation during the programming period*, Working Document No. 5, April.

——————— (2007n), Communication on Progressing Galileo: The Re-Profiling of the European GNSS Programmes, COM(2007) 534, Brussels, 19 September.

——————— (2007o), Communication Concerning the Revision of the Multi-annual Financial Framework (2007–13), COM(2007) 549, Brussels, 19 September.

——————— (2007p), *Growing Regions, Growing Europe, Fourth Report on Economic and Social Cohesion*, Official Publications of the European Communities, Luxembourg, May.

——————— (2007q), *Report from the Commission to the Council on the follow-up to 2005 Discharge Decisions (Summary) - Council Recommendations*, COM(2007) 537 final, Brussels, 19 September.

——————— (2007r), *Report from the Commission to the European Parliament on the follow-up to 2005 discharge decisions (summary)*, COM(2007) 538, and the attached Commission Working Document, SEC(2007) 1185, Brussels, 19 September.

——————— (2007s), "Reforming the Budget, Changing Europe: A Public Consultation Paper in View of the 2008/2009 Budget Review", Brussels, September.

European Convention (2002), Conclusions of the Working Group I on the Principle of Subsidiarity, CONV 286/02, Brussels, 23 September.

——————— (2003a), Contribution of Lord Tomlinson, "EU Budget: Building-in enhanced scrutiny of sound financial management", CONV 635/03, Brussels, 25 March.

——————— (2003b), "Discussion circle" on own resources: Response from Lord Tomlinson to the questions put to the Discussion Circle on Own Resources, Working Document 2, CONV 654/03, Brussels, 8 April.

——————— (2003c), "Discussion circle" on own resources: Note from Peter Hain, Member of the Convention – Comments on Secretariat Note describing the system of own resources (Cercle 3, WD 01), Working Document 4, Brussels, 11 April.

——————— (2003d), Proposal for an amendment to Art. III-311 of the draft Treaty submitted by Messrs Barnier, Vitorino, O'Sullivan and

Ponzano (retrieved from http://european-convention.eu.int/docs/treaty/pdf/892/Art%20III%20311%20Barnier%20FR.pdf).

———— (2003e), Contribution to the European Convention, Articles III.59 and III.60 in the draft EU Constitutional Treaty (submitted by P. Hain et al.), CONV 782/03, Brussels, 3 June.

European Council (1974), Meetings of the Heads of State or Government (Summit) in Paris, 9-10 December.

———— (1984), Conclusions of the Session of the European Council at Fontainebleau, 25-26 June.

———— (1992), Presidency Conclusions of the European Council in Edinburgh of 11-12 December, Doc/92/8, Brussels, December.

———— (1995), Presidency Note, "Progress Report on Statistics", 7057/95, Brussels, May.

———— (1998), Presidency Conclusions of the Cardiff European Council of 15-16 June, SN150/1/98 REV 1, Brussels, June.

———— (1999), Presidency Conclusions of the Berlin European Council of 24-25 March, SN 100/1/99, Brussels, March.

———— (2002), Presidency Conclusions of the Brussels European Council, 24-25 October, 14702/02, Brussels, November.

———— (2005a), *Financial Perspective 2007-2013,* 15915/05, Brussels, 19 December.

———— (2005b), Presidency Note, "Financial Perspective 2007–2013", 10090/05, Brussels, 15 June.

———— (2007a), Adoption of a Council Decision on the system of the European Communities' own resources (EC, Euratom), Commission Working Document on calculation, financing, payment and entry in the budget of the correction of budgetary imbalances, 9851/07 ADD 2, Brussels, 23 May.

———— (2007b), Presidency Conclusions of the Brussels European Council of 21-22 June, 11177/1/07 REV 1, Brussels, 20 July.

European Court of Auditors (1998), *Special Report No. 6/98 concerning the Court's assessment of the system of resources based on VAT and GNP*, OJ C 241, 31.7.1998.

————— (2000), *Special Report No. 17/2000 on the Commission's control of the reliability and comparability of the member states' GNP data*, OJ C 336, 27.11.2000.

————— (2004), *Annual Report concerning the financial year 2003*, OJ C 293, 30.11.2004.

————— (2005), *Annual Report concerning the financial year 2004*, OJ C 301, 30.11.2005.

————— (2006a), *Special Report No. 10/2006 on* ex post *evaluations of Objectives 1 and 3 programmes 1994 to 1999*, OJ C 302, 12.12.2006.

————— (2006b), *Annual Report concerning the financial year 2005*, OJ C 263, 30.10.2006.

————— (2007a), *Special Report No. 1/2007 concerning the implementation of the mid-term processes on the Structural Funds 2000–06*, OJ C 124, 5.6.2007.

————— (2007b), *Special Report No. 3/2007 concerning the management of the European Refugee Fund*, Luxembourg, OJ C 178, 31.7.2007.

————— (2007c), *Annual Report concerning the financial year 2006*, Luxembourg, November.

European Parliament (1985), *Report on behalf of the Committee on Budgets on the Commission's proposal for a Regulation extending the term of validity of Regulation No. 2892/77 and on the report from the Commission on the implementation of Council Regulations Nos. 2891/77 and 2892/77*, A2-126/85, Rapporteur: P. Cornelissen, 21 October.

————— (1994a), *Report on a New System of Own Resources for the European Union*, A3-0060/94, Rapporteur: H. Langes, 7 February.

————— (1994b), *Report on the System of Own Resources in the European Union*, A3-0228/94, Rapporteur: H. Langes, 8 April.

————— (2001), *Report on the situation concerning the European Union's own resources in 2001*, A5-0238/2001, Rapporteur: J. Haug, 26 June.

————— (2005a), Temporary Committee on Policy Challenges and Budgetary Means of the Enlarged Union 2007–13, Hearing with experts on 3 March 2005, Written contribution from: Prof. J. Krakowski, PE 355.430v01-00, March.

————— (2005b), *Report on Policy Challenges and Budgetary Means of the Enlarged Union 2007–2013*, A6-0153/2005, Temporary Committee on

Policy Challenges and Budgetary Means of the enlarged Union 2007-2013, Rapporteur: R. Böge, 19 May.

———— (2006), *Measurement of impact of structural actions on employment, quality of life and infrastructure: Relevant indicators*, April.

———— (2007a), *Annexes to the Explanatory Statement, Working Document No. 1 on the European Communities Own Resources*, A6-0066/2007, 13 March.

———— (2007b), *The Structural Funds' Implementation in Poland – Challenges for 2007–2013*, Budgetary Affairs, September.

European Parliament, Council and Commission (2006), Interinstitutional Agreement between the European Parliament, the Council and the Commission of 17 May 2006 on budgetary discipline and sound financial management, OJ C 139/1, 14.6.2006.

European Transport and Telecommunications Council (2002), Conclusions of the 2420th Council meeting, 7282/02, Brussels, 25–26 March.

Eurostat (1999), *Quality Work and Quality Assurance within Statistics*, 1999 edition, European Commission, Brussels.

Gerven, W. van (2007), "Political, ethical and financial and legal responsibility of EU Commissioners", Contribution presented at the public hearing on "Governance in the European Commission", European Parliament Committee on Budgetary Control, 3-4 October.

Giusta, P. (2006), *Ethics matters*, European Court of Auditors, Luxembourg.

Gretschmann, K. (1998), *Reform of the Own-Resources system and net positions in the EU budget*, Working Document, European Parliament, October.

Gros, D. and S. Micossi (2005), *A Better Budget for the European Union*, Policy Brief No. 66, CEPS, Brussels, February.

House of Commons, Select Committee on Foreign Affairs (1999), *Third Report*, Appendix 11, Supplementary Memorandum submitted by the Foreign and Commonwealth Office, London.

Hübner, D. (2007), "European Regional Policy: History, Achievements and Perspectives", Speech 07/542, Brussels, 17 September.

Jenkins, R. (1977), Speech by President Jenkins to the European Parliament, 11 January.

Kallas, S. (2006), Speech by the Vice-President of the European Commission responsible for Administrative Affairs, Audit and Anti-Fraud,

Commission's preliminary reply to the European Court of Auditors' Annual Report 2005 COCOBU, Speech/06/625, 23 October.

Le Cacheux, J. (2005), *Budget européen: le poison du juste retour*, Etudes et Recherches, No. 41, Notre Europe, Paris, June.

——— (2007), *Funding the EU Budget with a Genuine Own Resource: The Case for a European Tax*, Studies No. 57, Notre Europe, Paris, April.

Levy, R. (2003), "Confused Expectations: Decentralizing the Management of EU Programmes", *Public Money & Management Review*, Vol. 23, No. 2, April.

Mayhew, A. (2004), *The Financial Framework of the European Union, 2007–2013: New Policies? New Money?*, Working Paper No. 78, Sussex European Institute, University of Sussex, Brighton, October.

Marè, M. (2003), *La tassazione nell'Unione Europea: quale coordinamento? Quanta concorrenza?*, Rapporto di ricerca, Consiglio Nazionale dell'Economia e del Lavoro, Rome, July.

——— (2006), "A new VAT for the European Union: Taxing consumption and financing the budget", in G. Brosio and G. Muraro (eds), *Il Finanziamento del Settore pubblico*, Milan, F. Angeli.

Marè, M. and M. Sarcinelli (1991), "È l'Iva compatibile con il mercato unico del 1992?", *Politica Economica*, No. 2, August.

Metcalfe, L. (1992), "After 1992: Can the Commission Manage Europe?", *Australian Journal of Public Administration*, Institute of Public Administration Australia, Brisbane, March.

Neumann, V., O. Moez, X. Tschumi and M. Zarin-Nejadan (2004), *Effets économiques de l'aide publique au développement en suisse, Etude 2002*, DDC, Berne, December.

Pedone, A. (2003), "Il finanziamento del bilancio e i poteri di tassazione a livello europeo", mimeo, Sito del Servizio Consultivo ed Ispettivo Tributario, Rome, September.

Peet, J. and K. Ussher (1999), *The EU budget: An agenda for reform*, CER Pamphlet, Centre for European Reform, London.

Prodi, R. (1999), Address delivered to Parliament by Romano Prodi, President-Designate of the Commission on 21 July 1999, European Commission, Brussels.

——————— (2000a), "Shaping the New Europe", Speech to the European Parliament on 15 February 2000, Speech/00/41, European Commission, Brussels.

——————— (2000b), "White Paper on Reform", Speech by the President of the European Commission to the European Parliament, Plenary Session, 1 March 2000, Speech/00/62, European Commission, Brussels.

Reichenbach, H. (1983), « Les déséquilibres des flux budgétaires », *Revue Française de Finances Publiques*, No. 4.

Sinn, H.W. (1993), *How Much Europe? Subsidiarity, Centralization and Fiscal Competition*, Discussion Paper No. 834, Centre for Economic and Policy Research, London, September.

Santer, J. (1995), Speech by President Santer to the European Parliament, 17 January 1995, Speech/95/1, European Commission, Brussels.

——————— (1998), Speech to the European Parliament, 7 October 1998, European Commission, Brussels.

Sapir, A., P. Aghion, G. Bertola, M. Hellwig, J. Pisani-Ferry, D. Rosati, J. Viñals and H. Wallace (2003), *An agenda for a growing Europe: Making the EU economic system deliver*, Report of an independent High-Level Study Group established on the initiative of the President of the European Commission, Brussels, July.

Spaventa, L., P. Koopmans-Salmon, B. Spahn and S. Smith (1986), *The Future of Community Finance*, CEPS, Brussels.

Tabellini, G. (2002), "Principles of Policymaking in the European Union: An Economic Perspective", mimeo, October.

Tarschys, D. (2005), *The Enigma of European Added Value*, Swedish Institute for European Policy Studies, Stockholm, June.

Teutemann, M. (1992), *Rationale Kompetenzverteilung im Rahmen der europäischen Integration*, Berlin: Duncker & Humblot.